MW00399845

Environmentalism and the New Logic of Business

Environmentalism
and the New Logic of Business

*How Firms Can Be Profitable
and Leave Our Children a Living Planet*

R. EDWARD FREEMAN

JESSICA PIERCE

RICHARD DODD

OXFORD
UNIVERSITY PRESS
2000

OXFORD
UNIVERSITY PRESS

Oxford   New York

Athens   Auckland   Bangkok   Bogotá   Buenos Aires   Calcutta
Cape Town   Chennai   Dar es Salaam   Delhi   Florence   Hong Kong   Istanbul
Karachi   Kuala Lumpur   Madrid   Melbourne   Mexico City   Mumbai
Nairobi   Paris   São Paulo   Singapore   Taipei   Tokyo   Toronto   Warsaw

and associated companies in
Berlin   Ibadan

Published by Oxford University Press, Inc.
198 Madison Avenue, New York, New York 10016

Oxford is a registered trademark of Oxford University Press

Library of Congress Cataloging-in-Publication is available
ISBN 0-19-508093-9

1 3 5 7 9 8 6 4 2

Printed in the United States of America
on acid-free paper

For the Children
Ben, Emma, Molly, Kamalla,
Phoebe, Sebastien, Sage,
and others

Contents

Preface

The purpose of this book is to suggest how business can take a leadership role in the effort to improve our environment. Business can be green and profitable at the same time. Executives can rethink their corporate strategy in terms of four different "shades of green" to bring environmental innovations to their companies and their bottom lines.

Executives are treated to a daily barrage of conflicting reports about the state of the environment. Short of becoming an environmental scientist, how are managers to understand and act on this information? Is there an environmental crisis or not? We argue that we need to consider the consequences of being wrong about the environment, and the consequences to our children, especially. Having business play a leadership role in environmental affairs will help to assure a better future for our children and our companies. It is possible, but not easy, to be simultaneously profitable, green, and ethical.

This book began as a series of conversations among three people with diverse backgrounds: one, a philosopher interested in business; another, a religion scholar and environmentalist; a third, a student of management and later a consultant on environmental issues. We began with some naïve beliefs, which we still share. First, for the most part environmentalists and discussions of environmentalism have been hostile to the idea that business must be a large part of whatever answer we invent to solve our environmental problems. Second, business and ethics must go together.

And third, it is possible to craft methods and arguments to see capitalism in a new light, one that contains many shades of green.

Over the years many people have contributed to this project. We can only mention a few here. The BP Team in the Darden Class of 1991, Jamie Hendry, Tara Radin, Kristi Severance, Sarah Vogel, and Andrew Wicks have all contributed to the ideas and research on which this book is based. The members of the Commonweath Center for Literary and Cultural Change's seminar on Environmentalism and Culture stimulated much thinking and rewriting. The participants in the Environmental Ethics Doctoral Seminar at the Darden School in 1996 were instrumental in bringing to this book a conclusion, and Bill McDonough's students from all over the university in his Environmental Choices Seminar have offered helpful criticism for several terms. Hundreds of students and executives have listened and critiqued these ideas, and we are thankful to them especially if the results have some practical merit. Allen Beckenstein, Richard Brownlee, Alec Horniman, Andrea Larson, Joel Reichart, S. Venkatraman, Jack Weber, Patricia Werhane, and other Darden colleagues have always been willing to talk about these ideas with us. Jim Childress, William McDonough, and Jon Moreno have been their usual inspirational selves.

We have benefited from the support of several institutions and many people. We are grateful to the Darden School and the Darden Foundation, especially the Trustees and Deans John Rosenblum, Leo Higdon, and Ted Snyder, and Associate Dean Jim Freeland; the Olsson Center and its supporters—the Olsson family, the Ruffin Foundation, Wachovia Bank, British Petroleum, and others; and the Batten Center for Entrepreneurial Leadership. Herb Addison at Oxford University Press has been a supportive and wise editor on this project. Without his detailed attention and reading, this book would not be readable. A special thanks goes to the helpful and friendly staff at Gilbert and Teresa Lopez's Guadalajara and at Greenberry's of Charlottesville. Their patience for endless meals and coffee while we worked on this book is much appreciated. Without the daily inspiration of Kyosah-nims James and Virginia Hamrick and their students this project would have been abandoned.

We alone claim final responsibility for what is written here, to the relief of our friends, colleagues, and sponsors. And we realize that in trying to write a book that puts together what has been kept apart for a long time, we run the risk of pleasing no one. Philosophers and religion scholars will surely think that we are too deeply rooted in the practice of business. Environmentalists will claim that we have sold out to capitalism. Executives will insist that we have not paid enough attention to the competitive needs of business and to the balancing of business needs with environmental caution. If the truth be told, we didn't write this book for any of these groups. We wrote it for the children.

R.E.F., J.P., R.D.
Charlottesville, Omaha, London
1999

Environmentalism and the New Logic of Business

CHAPTER ONE

Shades of Green
A New Approach

Introduction

Edgar Woolard, former chairman of E. I. du Pont de Nemours and Company, spoke at a conference of environmentalists, business students, and business academics about the difficulty of implementing strict new pollution standards. DuPont, long seen as a big polluter and a favorite target of environmentalists, had worked extremely hard to clean up its act and had recently announced a commitment to zero pollution. Woolard recalled a story about a plant that was not able to meet the new environmental standards. The plant engineers assured Woolard that there was no way the plant could be changed to meet the new standards, so Woolard suggested that the plant would have to be closed. Several weeks later the engineers reappeared with a solution. When Woolard asked them how much the solution would cost, they sheepishly replied that the new methods would actually save money.[1]

The Challenge of Business Leadership Today

It is possible for business leaders to make money, do the right thing, and participate in saving the earth. It is possible, but it is not easy.

This book begins a conversation about how business, ethics, and the environment can come together.[2] However, we have to warn you that we don't have any quick solutions, magic bullets, or

1

foolproof formulas for success. Instead we are going to show you how to begin to understand the concepts involved in business, ethics, and the environment. We are going to suggest how you and your organization can begin to ask the right questions.

This is a book about possibilities. Instead of showing the myriad ways that business, ethics, and the environment conflict and lead to impossible choices, we are going to ask the question, How is it possible to put these ideas together?[3] In today's world, as well as the one we are creating for our children, all three are necessary. Our businesses must continue to create value for their financiers and other stakeholders. In an interconnected global economy we can no longer afford the ethical excesses that many see as characteristic of the last several decades. And, if we are to leave a livable world for our children and their children, we simply must pay attention to environmental matters. Yet most of the methods, concepts, ideas, theories, and techniques that we use in business do not pull business, ethics, and the environment together. From discounted cash flow to human resources planning, neither ethics nor the environment is central to the way we think about business.

Everyone shares the joke about the very idea of "business ethics" as an oxymoron—two words whose juxtaposition is contradictory. Much of business language is oriented toward seeing a conflict between business and ethics. We routinely juxtapose profits with ethics, as if making an ethical decision costs profits.[4] We sometimes qualify difficult choices that distribute harms and benefits to communities and employees as "business decisions," signaling that business and ethics are not thought to be compatible.[5]

The environment fares no better. It is seen as a necessary evil, a cost to be minimized, or a regulation with which to comply. We almost never think about the environment as central to the main metaphors of business, its strategic and people management systems, unless, of course, there is some regulation that constrains business strategy, a mess to be cleaned up, or a public issue that pits executives against environmentalists. Historically, businesspeople have not been encouraged to get involved with environmental concerns or have been discouraged from doing so. Our models and theories of business have traditionally been silent on the subject of the environment. However, the world of the next century will hear a great deal of noise.

More and more citizens see themselves as environmentalists. Governments are increasing their cooperative actions to address global environmental concerns such as global warming and biodiversity. Interest groups are beginning to propose solutions to problems that involve business decision making outside of and beyond government regulation.

What we desperately need are new ideas, concepts, and theories that allow us to think about business, ethics, and the environment in one full breath. We need to see these issues coming together rather than conflicting. Today's challenge to business leadership is sustaining profitability, doing the right thing, *and* being green. This book is about how to accept and respond to this challenge.

The Environment: It's Everywhere

Early in the morning of March 24, 1989, the supertanker EXXON *Valdez* ran aground on Bligh Reef in Prince William's Sound off the coast of Alaska. In the days following the accident every action or inaction by EXXON executives, government officials, and environmentalists was subjected to unprecedented public scrutiny.[6]

In addition to damaging the ecosystem, the Valdez spill symbolizes an important milestone in business history. The environment is an issue that has come to stay. It is not a fad, a passing fancy, or the issue of the day.

There is not a single aspect of our world today that can escape the scrutiny of environmental analysis. Pollution of air, water, and land, the production and disposal of hazardous wastes, solid waste disposal, chemical and nuclear spills and accidents, global warming and the greenhouse effect, ozone depletion, deforestation and desertification, biodiversity, and overpopulation are a few of the issues that today's executive needs to understand to be environmentally literate.

We are treated to daily doom and gloom press reports about the state of the earth. Scientists have "discovered" that global warming is or is not a problem, is or is not caused by solar storms, is or is not related to the emission of greenhouse gases, and so forth. We want to know the answer, the whole truth, "just the facts," about the environment, and we get disturbed by so many conflicting reports.[7]

The truth is that there is no one truth about the environment. The truth is that we have not lived in a way that respects the environment and preserves it for our children's children.

Barriers to a Green Conversation

If we are going to explore how we can rethink business along an environmental dimension, and if the outcome of this conversation is to include many different ways of creating and sustaining value, then we must be on the lookout for barriers that will prevent us from engaging the tough issues. These barriers are produced by our inability to entertain new ideas: our mind-set. We have identified five mind-sets. They all say that our project—integrating business, ethics, and the environment into new modes of thinking—is impossible. We say more about action and barriers to action in chapter 5.

The Regulatory Mind-set

This mind-set sees the environment as a part of the business government relationship to be spelled out in terms of regulation or public policy. The regulatory mind-set says that the best way to take care of the environment is through the public policy process that produces laws and rules with which business must comply. It discounts the possibility and the wisdom of voluntary initiatives that stem from deeply held environmental values, or even the desire to respond to the environmental preferences. Although the recent history of concern with the environment has usually meant passing laws and their attendant regulations, the debate today goes far beyond a regulatory mind-set. Regulation lags behind the real world, and regulation inevitably entails unforeseen consequences.

Our question for the regulatory mind-set is, Are you confident that government, as it currently works, will create a sustainable future for your children?

The Cost-Benefit Mind-set

The cost-benefit mind-set is sometimes related to the regulatory mindset simply because many regulatory regimes use cost-benefit methods to determine "proper" regulations. The cost-benefit mind-set says that cleaning up the environment or making products and services more environmentally friendly has costs and benefits. And we should go only as far as the benefits outweigh the costs.

There are several problems with this view. The first is that if you focus on costs and benefits you will fail to use "innovation." The argument is similar to the quality approach. By focusing on the cost of quality, managers make wrong decisions. Instead by focusing on quality processes like six sigma quality, human innovation takes over and drives quality up and costs down. The cost-benefit mind-set says that there is a contradiction between "environmentally friendly" and costs. Many companies that adopt one or more of the shades of green that we recommend are making money and becoming more environmentally friendly. By focusing on costs and benefits, managers are inevitably led to ask the wrong questions.

The second problem with the cost-benefit mind-set is that it assumes one particular set of underlying values: economic ones. Many environmentalists, executives, and other thinkers have questioned the priority of our current ways of thinking about economics. All value is not economic value, and anyone who believes that is trying to get us to live in a certain way. Does the last gorilla have just an economic value? What about the beauty of the Grand Tetons? What about the future of our children? Human life is rich and complex and is not reducible solely to an economic calculation. It is degrading to all of us to think that we only value people and things in simple economic terms.

The Constraint Mind-set

Many argue that the main purpose of business is to create and sustain economic value, and everything else from ethics to the environment to meaningful work is best viewed as a side constraint. The business of business is business. Anything else is to be viewed as not the main objective of business.

There is a nugget of truth here, as there is in each of these prevalent mind-sets. Economic value has been the main focus of business, and other kinds of value have been seen as constraining a kind of unfettered capitalism that is driven by the urge to win, succeed, and compete. However, a more thoughtful analysis of "economic value creation" shows that it is impossible to separate out "economic, political, social, personal" aspects of value. When the employees of Delta Airlines buy a jet for the company, when Johnson and Johnson recalls Tylenol, when Body Shop employees volunteer to help the homeless, when Mattel donates money to a riot-torn part of Los Angeles, all of these actions imply a company can be driven by economics and by ethics. We are not arguing that economics is unimportant but that reducting all human value creation–value sustaining activity to economic measures misses the mark. Business does more, as Adam Smith realized, and to reduce capitalism to a narrow view of economics endangers our free society.[8]

The Sustainable Development Mind-set

It may seem strange to categorize what is supposed to be a way to save the earth with mind-sets that prevent environmental progress. Obviously not all discussions of sustainable development act as barriers, but one recent discussion simply misses the mark. The Brundtland Report, the basis of the 1992 Rio Earth Summit, called on governments to redefine economic activity to become sustainable. The problem with this view is that it calls on governments to play an intrusive role in the process of value creation, but if we have learned anything from the collapse of state socialism, governments and centralized approaches do not work very well. Ultimately, a worldwide regime of environmental coop-eration could become a threat to democratic freedom, especially if combined with the other mind-sets. Decisions on the future of whole industries and companies could become a matter of gov-ernment beliefs about what is sustainable.

Recall our view that there is no one truth about the environ-ment. We believe that it is necessary to adopt a radically decentral-ized approach that focuses on shared values, and a conversation about those shared values. If such an approach is not viable, then we should see the heavy hand of the state as part and parcel of our failure to integrate business, ethics, and the environment.

The Greenwashing Mind-set

The greenwashing mind-set pervades many discussions of the environment.[9] Characteristic of it is the view that business could never act on values other than profit maximization. Whenever we see a company engaged in something that seems to be good for the environment, we should be deeply skeptical. Truth be told, the company is probably trying to make money, avoid some future cost, or engage in other narrowly self-interested schemes. Many environmental programs at companies are, on this view, cleverly disguised attempts to be seen as green while really continuing in an environmentally destructive mode.

As we have presented these ideas to groups of people who are deeply committed to environmental values but have little real contact with the inner workings of business, there has been an assumption that "business is bad."[10] Now it is surely true that there are attempts to greenwash—portray trivial changes to prod-ucts, services, and processes in grand and glorious environmental terms. And we should always examine such claims carefully. However, the assumption that therefore all business attempts at environmental action are suspect simply does not follow.

We want to suggest that we be skeptical of all grand environ-mental claims, whether they be from business, government, envi-ronmental groups, or scientists. The arena is very uncertain and complex. However, the greenwash mindset makes our task impossible, so we shall set it aside. Of course, businesses want to make money, but it doesn't follow that the environment must be left out of the equation, or that profit is the only value which counts. In chapter 2 we outline a view of business that we believe is literally sweeping the world—a view in which values are the driving force.

Our Children's Future: A Wager

The seventeenth-century French philosopher Blaise Pascal formulated an interesting argument supporting the rationality of belief in the Christian God. He suggested that if Christianity were essentially true, then someone who did not believe was destined for an eternity in hell. But if Christianity were essentially false, someone who lived according to Christian principles would lose little or nothing. This argument, entitled "Pascal's wager," has been the subject of much discussion and debate over the years.[11] We want to suggest that there is a "Pascal's wager on the environment" that goes like this.

Let's assume an optimistic scenario which implies that the gloomy forecasts are all wrong. Maybe there is enough room for landfills for generations to come. Global warming may be elusive. Many chemicals may well be harmless. The destruction of forests may be insignificant and well worth the benefits of development. Clean and healthful water may someday be plentiful. And perhaps we can invent the technology we need to compensate for whatever damage we have actually done to the earth.

Are you willing to bet the future of your children on this optimistic scenario? If it is wrong or even partially wrong with respect to, say, "global warming," then there will be no inhabitable world left for our children. As in Pascal's wager, we are going to assume that it is reasonable to bet that there is in fact an environmental crisis. The consequences of being wrong are too great to bet otherwise.

Yet the great majority of responses to the environmental crisis have been at best ineffective. The main response mode has been to marshal the public policy process to legislate that the air and water be cleaner and to assign the costs of doing so to states, localities, and businesses. Twenty-plus years of environmental regulation in the United States has led to "environmental gridlock." There is disagreement and contention at several important levels.

First, as we stated earlier, there isn't any one truth about the state of the environment. Many (but not all) individual scientific "facts" are disputable. There is widespread disagreement about the scientific answers to environmental questions and even about how the questions should be stated.[12]

Second, even those who agree about the science of a particular issue still disagree about the appropriate public policy. Even if we agree that greenhouse gases lead to global warming, we may well disagree that limiting carbon dioxide emissions to 1998 levels will solve the problem.

Third, there is disagreement about underlying values. How should we live? By exploiting the earth's resources? By conserving the earth's resources? By living with nature? Should we be vegetarians to improve the ability of advanced societies to feed the hungry and use land efficiently? Should we recycle or should we consume green products or should we build an ethic of anticonsumption—of saving the earth rather than consuming it?

These three levels of disagreement lead to gridlock, especially in a public policy process that purports to base policy on facts rather than values. Overlay these three levels of disagreement on a litigious system of finding, blaming, and punishing polluters of the past and the result is a conversation about the environment that goes nowhere fast.[13]

We believe that this public policy process needs to change and that we need to have a better conversation about the environment and the role of governments. In chapter 5 we make some suggestions about how to have a better conversation. But we are not willing to wait for these changes to take place. Instead we want to suggest another mode of response to the environmental crisis: business strategy. If we can come to see how business activity can take place, systematically, in environmentally friendly ways, then we can respond to the environmental crisis in lasting and effective ways.[14]

The Basics of Business: What You Stand For

At the thousands of McDonald's franchises around the world one thing is the same: QVC—quality, value, and cleanliness. McDonald's is built around realizing these values. This is why at any McDonald's anywhere you get good quality fast food, a clean restaurant, and a good comparative price. The very meaning of McDonald's encompasses these values, and everyone from CEO to fry cook has to understand their job in terms of these values.[15]

Strangely enough, a tiny company, only a fraction of the size of McDonald's works the same way. The company is called Johnsonville Sausage in Johnsonville and Sheboygan, Wisconsin, It is highly profitable, is growing fast, and works on values that differ from McDonald's. At Johnsonville Sausage the operating philosophy is self-improvement. The company exists in order for the individuals in it to realize their goals and to continue to improve themselves. Values drive Johnsonville Sausage and many other businesses in today's fast-changing world.[16]

There is a revolution afoot in business—a revolution with "values" at its core. It was sparked by Tom Peters and Bob Waterman's best-selling *In Search of Excellence*, the rediscovery of Edward Demming's ideas on the productive workplace and the role of values and quality. Countless programs for individual and organizational change have been ignited by an increasingly competitive global marketplace; business today is turning to values.[17]

At one level this emphasis on values cuts against the traditions of business. It has always been assumed that business promotes only one primary value—profits. Both the academic research and the how-to advice books on business are full of ideas on how to become more profitable. And profits are the lifeblood of business. But surely the purpose of life is not just to breathe or keep our hearts beating. Humans are capable of more, of standing for principles, of caring for others, or creating value for ourselves and others. Even those few people who care only for themselves must avoid trampling on the rights and projects of others.

Organizations are no different. Profits are important, necessary—add any words you want—but there is more. Businesses can and often do stand for something more than profitability. Some, like IBM, stand for creating value for customers, employees, and shareholders. Others, like Merck, stand for the alleviation of human suffering. Still others, like Mesa Petroleum, may well stand for creating value for shareholders only; but even those companies must do so within the confines of the law and of public expectations that could be turned into law.

This concern for values can be summarized in the idea of enterprise strategy, or asking the question, What do you stand for? The typical strategy process in a company asks someone to think about the following questions: (1) What business are we in? (2) What is our competitive advantage in this business? (3) How can we sustain competitive advantage? (4) What product/market focus should we take? (5) What needs to change in order to be successful? Some of these questions go into every company's architecture of its portfolio of businesses. Even small businesses have to have some business plan, perhaps in the mind of the entrepreneur, which articulates how that small business creates, captures, and sustains value.

For this values revolution in business to be meaningful, a prior question must be considered, the question of enterprise strategy: What do you stand for? A business's answer to this question sets forth a statement of the core values of the organization and provides a context in which the strategy questions mentioned earlier can be answered.[18] For instance, if you stand for human dignity and some basic idea of human rights for all, then there are probably some markets that you will not serve, and some products and services that you will not provide. If you stand for quality, cleanliness, and value, then there are certain business opportunities that you will forego because you cannot produce the quality service, cannot produce it in a clean environment, or cannot provide it at a price that gives good value.

All of this may sound rather fanciful, but the basic point is that businesses have discovered that articulating some bedrock—some foundation, some basic values—has enormous benefits. The business becomes focused around these values. People, from executives to mail clerks, begin to believe in them or may be attracted to the firm because of these values. In short, business strategy makes more sense in the context of values.

Indeed the logic of values provides the very engine of business. Far from the inhibiting mind-sets that we mentioned earlier, the innovation mind-set is central to thinking creatively about business. Employees who believe in values are moved to innovate to realize those values. When the organization is committed to realizing the values, then the values become all-important. People will try anything if it helps them realize what's important to them. We'll have more to say about the importance of this innovation mind-set in the next chapter.

It is easy to see how thinking about the environment, and about ethics, is compatible with the values revolution. By clearly stating and understanding the core beliefs that an organization has or wants to adopt about ethical issues such as honesty, integrity, dignity of individuals, caring about others, and so on, policies that are straightforward and easily implementable can be designed. By clearly thinking through a position on the environment, whether it just complies with the law or tries to leave the earth in better condition, we can begin to marshal resources to realize these basic beliefs.

Executives can begin to meet the challenge of leadership that we articulated earlier—being profitable, doing the right thing, and helping to save the earth—by understanding and articulating an enterprise strategy, an answer to the question, What do we stand for? In chapter 3 we outline this process in more detail. For now it is enough to mention that lots of companies are doing this today, and it works. From huge DuPont to little Ben and Jerry's, from oil and chemical companies to retail boutiques, articulating what you stand for on the environment is step one to a greener world, one that we can pass along to our children.

Shades of Green

There are many strategies that businesses can adopt which are more friendly toward the environment, four primary "shades of green," each having its own logic and admitting many interpretations. Let's call these shades (1) light green, (2) market green, (3) stakeholder green, and (4) dark green. You can think of these shades as phases of development in a company's strategy, moving from light green to dark green, but keep in mind that each shade has its own logic and it isn't necessary to move from one shade to the next. Each shade offers its own way to create and sustain value, so that business, ethics, and the environment go together. We'll offer more details about each shade of green in chapter 3, but here's a thumbnail sketch of the logic of each shade of green.

Light green, or "legal green," is a shade with which most companies are familiar. Being light green involves complying with the following principle: *Create and sustain competitive advantage by ensuring that your company is in compliance with the law.* The logic of light green relies on the public policy process to drive its strategy. But it is a mistake to think that no competitive advantage is possible, since every company has to obey the law. That idea is mistaken on two counts.

First, as Michael Porter and his colleagues have argued, countries with strict environmental standards seem to gain an edge in global marketplaces—they become more efficient and have better technology.[19] Second, within an industry, companies can actively pursue public policies that fit with their special competitive advantage. By innovating with technology and know-how, a company gains an advantage over a competitor who cannot comply as efficiently. Light green thinking thus creates the possibility for competitive advantage.

Market green logic focuses on customers rather than on the public policy process. The following principle is at work: *Create and sustain competitive advantage by paying attention to the environmental preferences of customers.*

Market green strategies are based on "the greening of the customer," a fast-growing and controversial phenomenon. Today's customer-focused, market-driven company cannot afford to miss the fact that customers prefer environmentally friendly products— without added costs. Clearly, creating and sustaining competitive advantage is a matter of "better, cheaper, faster." Companies that can meet these environmental needs will be the winners. Customer perceptions about the company's "shade of green" are crucial, but, most importantly, the products and services have to perform.

Market green logic applies good, old-fashioned "smell the customer" thinking to the environment. Note that this may or may not be in conjunction with legal green. Market green logic roots competitive advantage in customer needs and the ability of the customer-driven company to deliver on these needs. There is nothing unusual except giving up the costly belief that environmentally friendly products always entail higher costs and competitive disadvantages. Notice that market green logic can apply in the industrial sector as well as the consumer sector and to services as well as products. We'll say more about these distinctions in chapter 3.

Stakeholder green is a shade darker than market green. It applies market green logic to key stakeholder groups such as customers, suppliers, employees, communities, shareholders, and other financiers. There are many different ways to slice the stakeholder pie. Companies can seek to maximize the benefits of one group or they can seek to harmonize the interests of all groups. We'll say more about this in chapter 2. Stakeholder green gets its color from responding to the needs of some or all stakeholder groups. It obeys the following principle: *Create and sustain competitive advantage by responding to the environmental preferences of stakeholders.*

Stakeholder green strategies are based on a more thoroughgoing adoption of environmental principles to all aspects of a company's operations. Many companies have adopted a version of stakeholder green by requiring suppliers to meet environmental requirements and by setting strict standards for the manufacturing process. Paying attention to recyclable material in consumer packaging, educating employees on environmental issues, participating in community efforts to clean up the environment, and appealing to investors who want to invest in green companies are all a part of stakeholder green. This shade does not require one or a focused set of actions but does require anticipating and responding to a whole set of issues in regard to the environment. As such it is more complicated than the lighter shades. The logic of stakeholder green is similar to the logic of quality processes. Unless quality processes permeate a company at all levels, they are doomed to fail. There are different levels of commitment to stakeholder green, just as there are different levels of commitment to quality, but any effective commitment must be pervasive.

Dark Green is a shade for which few companies strive. Being dark green commits a company to being a leader in making environmental principles a fundamental basis of doing business. Dark green suggests the following principle: *Create and sustain value in a way that sustains and cares for the earth.*

To most businesspeople this principle sounds idealistic or fanciful, which shows how much we have ignored the environment in our thinking about business. Indigenous peoples know that this principle must be obeyed because they live close to the land. We teach our children to care for their things and those things, such as our homes and land, that we share. It does not require a large leap of the imagination to expect that the same values are possible in business.

Dark green logic is not antibusiness, though many people believe it is. Humans create value for each other, and "business" is the name we have given to that process. Dark green logic says that we must respect and care for the earth in this process of value creation. How to spell out what respect and care imply is an important task, which we undertake in chapter 3.

There are more than four shades of green. Indeed, you can invent your own shade for your company. Look at these four as anchors that can define what is possible for your company. Dark green is not for everyone, and light green may well be universal. Dark green raises more questions than it answers, for it reminds us that the very idea of "living with the earth" or "treating the earth with respect" are difficult issues that bring forth deep philosophical questions.

We are not trying to define the optimal shade for everyone; our argument is that *variation is good*. Imagine a world in which there

15

are thousands of enterprises trying to realize competitive advantage through environmental means. Undoubtably, many of these innovations will fail, but some will succeed, and many will lead to other, more important innovations. It is only through a large-scale process of many small innovations that real, lasting change can occur. Perhaps while such innovation is emerging, someone, somewhere, will invent a revolutionary "pollution machine" that will cure all of our environmental ills, or some official will "discover" the perfect set of regulations. All well and good if that happens, but we are suggesting a more modest and, we believe, more workable approach.

Understanding Environmentalism

Ultimately how we run our companies reflects our commitment to how we want to live. Our values are lived through our behavior. Someone who espouses "green values" but does nothing to realize those values lives in bad faith or self-deception. "Bad faith" means that we say one thing and do another, and "self-deception" means that we are not honest with ourselves about what we truly believe and how we really want to live. Ethics, in life and in business, starts with an assumption of good faith and self-awareness, or at least an acknowledgment of the difficulties involved in being authentic to our true beliefs.

Nowhere do we see these issues more plainly than in environmentalism and environmental values. Talk is cheap, and its price is related to a shared history and culture of not living in a way that guarantees our children a future. We believe that there are many ways to live—indeed, many ways to live in an environmentally sustainable way—but we also know that our values have not always led us in any sustainable direction.

Environmentalism is one expression of the responsibility that we have to live ethically. Environmentalism and environmentalists come in many guises. If executives are to adopt shades of green, they must understand the value bases of environmentalists and environmentalism. In contrast to the mind-sets that prevent firms from becoming environmentally active, there are three mind-sets that motivate environmentalism and environmentalists. We are not identifying one of these as the correct one, but executives need to understand all three.

Environmentalists with a conservation mind-set tell us to conserve the earth's resources for the future. This view of environmentalism is a minimal response to our children's wager.

Environmentalists with a social justice mind-set tell us that there are many ways to improve the institutions that we have created. These environmentalists focus on those who have been mistreated by those institutions—women, minorities, and indigenous peoples—and traces a connection between their mistreatment and our view of the environment.

Environmentalists with a deep ecology mind-set ask us to view the earth as a living organism and to find a way to talk about the earth and its creatures in our human-centered moral discourse. We should live in a way that is sustainable and self-renewing rather than destructive of current resources.

Each of these three mind-sets challenges our ways of doing business. It is easiest to integrate conservation-minded environmentalists with the normal ways we think about business, but we shall argue that what is necessary to meet our children's future is a conversation that takes all three kinds of environmentalists into account.

The Plan of the Book

In the chapters that follow we try to spell out our four shades of green in detail and explain the arguments for adopting a greener point of view in business. In chapter 2 we examine the new logic of business that is values driven and suggest that green values can be an important part of the equation. In chapter 3 we elaborate on the four shades of green and include some methods that you can use to see where your company fits. In chapter 4 we argue that if a company is going to adopt a shade of green, then it must understand the underlying values of both environmentalists and environmentalism. In chapter 5 we outline a program for change in organizations, and we offer some suggestions for a "green conversation" in our society that redefines the role of business, government, and the individual citizen. We have included in the appendix some basic information about the argument that an environmental crisis does in fact exist.

Summary

We want to engage you in a conversation about how to think about business, ethics, and the environment together rather than separately. We are confident that the results of this conversation can make a difference—to us and to our children. If you are confident that your children have a safe and secure future, then you don't need to wrestle with the questions that this conversation raises and you don't need to examine your values and behavior to see if changes need to be made. But we do not share your confidence.

We do not have confidence that the future is secure, nor do we have confidence that our current institutions, as well-meaning as they may be, are doing all that is necessary. We are confident that if we can begin to think about business in environmentally sound ways, we can make real progress. We shall ask difficult questions and suggest some nontraditional answers. Our goal is to challenge you to formulate your own environmental principles and ultimately to formulate your own answer to our children's wager.[20]

CHAPTER TWO

Environmentalism
and the New Logic of Business

The New Logic of Business

It is an understatement to say that the last thirty years have produced a multiplicity of changes in business. Every day new management gurus appear to tell executives how to cope with change, how to understand change, how to value change, even how to change themselves and their families.

Capitalism is built on a logic of change. Someone, or perhaps a group, figures out a better way to do something, or someone creates a new idea or a new gadget, and the effects are to make the old way of doing things different or obsolete. Economist Joseph Schumpeter called this process "creative destruction" and claimed that it was the heart of capitalism. Thus, the idea that the logic of business is the logic of change is not new.

Why then does business feel differently today? In the past most businesses had to worry about conditions in one or a few countries in the world, and methods of communication were relatively slow. Today, executives in most companies must understand what is happening around the world, and communication is instantaneous.

There are few barriers between countries, especially with respect to the movement of capital. Capital markets are truly global and political institutions around the world are increasingly liberal. As capital markets have become freer, so too have political institutions.[1] Add the incredible explosion of information technology to the mix and the new logic of business isn't just change, it's chaos.[2]

The old logic of business proceeded at a rate whereby change could be self-renewing and relatively stable. It's not that there was no or little change but that the managerial systems were regulated by the amount of change. For example, the automobile companies in the United States planned, organized, led, and controlled the process of creative destruction called "planned obsolescence." The entire system was stable and self-renewing, and it could cope with lots of changes that appeared in the form of new models of products every twelve months. Access to this market by others, the enormous capital requirements, and so on, were all barriers to competitors. These barriers have been broken down and overcome, however, and now the industry is in a state of chaos, relative to the earlier model.

Consider the plight of IBM and others in the computer industry, introducing generation after generation of new and improved mainframes. Then a combination of readily available capital, entrants from all over the world, a new software industry, and the Internet made the orderly process of creative destruction come unglued.

In short, the new logic of business is paradoxical. In the old order managers could plan, organize, lead, and control, but in the new order there is no such luxury. Business executives today must think both globally and locally. There must be some logic that ties together operations (or even lack of operations) all over the world from Jakarta to London to Omaha. But that same logic must be sensitive to differing conditions, different cultures, and different markets all over the globe. Businesses today are held together by increasingly sophisticated centralized control systems, but organizational structures are becoming increasingly decentralized, clouding traditional lines of authority and responsibility. Gone are the many levels and layers of management and staff that could rationally manage differences, replaced by process owners who sometimes cut across business units and multiple interfaces all over the world held together by that most precious of all commodities in today's world: information. Thus, executives must centralize and decentralize at the same time.

Executives today must show leadership, but leadership is different from the traditional bureaucratic-military model. Leadership must include the idea that those closest to the work know best how to do it. The old command and control style is no longer appropriate. Thus, we need both strong leadership and empowerment at the same time.

Finally, amid restructuring and reengineering, downsizing and rightsizing—amid all of the chaos—executives must convince people to come to work with their hearts. A workforce that is not committed 100 percent to the goals of the joint enterprise—the corporation—is destined for the unpleasant and swift side of the process of creative destruction. We need both continuous restructuring and employee commitment.

The Role of Environmentalism

Another important paradox to emerge in the new logic of business is the paradox of being green and being profitable. For many years companies believed that environmental issues could be managed if everyone in the industry were forced to incur similar costs. Environmentalism came at a price, which was paid by all in proportion to their market power and position. In a sense environmental costs could be treated as a pass-through to the consumer. The new logic of business changes that thinking. Being green by being more expensive is simply unacceptable today for at least two reasons.

First, companies today face competitive pressures from the entire world. Everyone is not playing by the same rules. Environmental standards differ around the world. To gain real and sustainable competitive advantage, companies have to innovate and not simply address environmental issues by adding to the cost curve.

Second, and more important, we are uncertain about "the environmental facts." We argued in chapter 1 that the uncertainty was high enough and the consequences were important enough that it is irrational to believe that there is no environmental crisis, regardless of the facts. We suggested that Pascal's wager for the environment was a sound one for the sake of our children. This means that we have to rethink our businesses in environmental terms. Taking the easy road by adding to the cost curve won't meet the challenge.

The Need for Stakes in the Ground

The paradoxes of business call for a new logic, a new approach, to business, one that is grounded in values. The question facing business is whether or not it can be based on a set of values that help manage the paradoxes. By returning to the basics (and values are the most basic ideas around), we want to suggest that the old story of business needs revision.

The Old Story: Cowboy Capitalism

It is standard thinking in businesses and business schools that the only business value is profit. More profits mean that a business is better positioned for survival in the tough competitive battlefield. Business metaphors are taken from warfare and violence. New product introductions are competitive battles, employees are the troops, and competitors are the enemy. Any stakeholder that gets in the way of winning the war, such as government regulatory agencies or environmentalists, are to be pacified so that we can get on with the real business of business: winning the war against competitors.

We might call this overromanticized view of business "cowboy capitalism" because it imitates our view of the "taming of the west" by the rough-and-tumble cowboys depicted on American television shows of the past few decades. That the language of cowboy capitalism permeates business *and* theories about business is plain. However, it is equally obvious that such language is no more than a twisted half-truth about what really goes on in business.

Business is not, for the most part, a series of singular encounters between enemies. Most businesses, even in the highly competitive arena of capital markets, serve customers over time, with many repeat encounters. Most businesses, even in low-wage industries, want employees who are committed to the organization and are willing to spend some of their human capital to make the organization successful.

Focusing on the rhetoric of competition tends to obscure these more basic truths about business. We believe that the rhetoric of cowboy capitalism is destructive. Surely, we all know that competition is necessary to capitalism. But cowboy capitalism assumes that businesses are not only competitive but that the cowboys are only self-interested and willing (and justified) to do anything that wins the war.

For an example of the destructiveness of the story, look at the emergence of cowboy capitalism in countries that had been ravaged by the ills of state socialism. By adopting what these societies understood as capitalism, they created systems of widespread cheating, deceit, and greed. Ironically these former socialists have come to believe *and practice* their own socialist ideas about what capitalism is as a system. Cowboy capitalism has been adopted in full force in the former Soviet Union.

In this old, worn-out story environmentalism doesn't play much of a role. It is something to be fought against, lobbied against, and resisted at all costs lest it constrain the "freedom" of the cowboys to do whatever they like.

What is necessary is the emergence of a new story—one that places competition in its proper place, as an emergent property of business rather than a fundamental basic. This new story must allow business to act on values in order to create profit. This new story must find a central place for environmental values rather than see them as merely constraining forces. It is only in this new story that we have a chance to put together business, ethics, and the environment.

The New Story: Values-Based Capitalism

We want to call this new, emerging story of business "values-based capitalism" or perhaps "stakeholder capitalism."[3] The terms are new, but the story has actually been enacted for some time, since the lens of cowboy capitalism does not allow us to see it. Values-based capitalism depends on four key principles: stakeholder cooperation, complexity, continuous creation, and emergent competition.

The first principle of values-based capitalism is that capitalism depends first and foremost on the cooperation of stakeholders. The job of the entrepreneur or manager is to put together a deal so that customers, employees, suppliers, financiers, and communities win over time. Without the support of each of these groups, firms are not viable. Indeed there is a great deal of evidence that companies which endure over time and perform at a very high level understand and practice this principle.[4]

The second principle of values-based capitalism is that people are complex. This statement may seem pedestrian, but, astoundingly, the assumptions of the old story deny this simple truth. Cowboy capitalism assumes that most people are one-dimensional maximizers incapable of acting beyond their narrow self-interest.[5] Clearly, people do sometimes act selfishly, but they often act for others. Most of the time, they do neither and instead pursue *joint conceptions of the good*, which may be called shared values. From the early views of Peters and Waterman (*In Search of Excellence*) to calls for sustainable development by authors such as Paul Hawken, acting on shared values is necessary if business is to work. Merck has been a great company *because* it has believed in alleviating suffering. Johnson and Johnson has performed well *because* its business associates see the famous Credo in action. And the list of such companies is growing longer.[6] All of these companies could be described as fierce competitors. And it is the activation of values that creates such "fierceness."

The third principle of values-based capitalism can be called "continuous creation." This twist on Schumpeter's principle of creative destruction that one innovation must destroy a previous one is meant to emphasize that capitalism is mainly creative rather than mainly destructive. Of course, some of the creative force of capitalism destroys the value previously created, but only in theory does this happen immediately. Most of the creative force of capitalism in fact coexists with what it purportedly "destroys." If firm A invents a product or improves a product that firm B depends on, firm B is not destroyed; rather, it creates yet another innovation. Creativity is a continuous process of capitalism, especially where the drive to create is caused by people trying to realize and act on those things that are most important to them: their values.

The fourth principle of values-based capitalism is the principle of emergent competition. This principle says that when capitalism is found in a society with relatively free political institutions, competition emerges from the first three principles.[7] Where social and political institutions provide relatively easy access to customers, suppliers, financiers, employees, and communities, then inventors, entrepreneurs, and other value creators can challenge the established order.

We want to suggest that this new story of capitalism is a bold and powerful edifice. It says that businesses are successful because people stand for some values and that stakeholder deals exist and are relatively stable because most people keep their contracts, promises, and commitments. In short, it provides the possibility of a framework for understanding business strategy in a very different light.

Toward a New Framework

If what we have said about the role of values and capitalism makes sense, then we need to take the next step and outline the implications of values-based capitalism for corporate executives and for business strategy.

The old story of cowboy capitalism couches questions of business strategy in warlike metaphors, for example, what battlefield are we playing on? What is the alignment of our resources (armies)? But these metaphors have given way to strategic planning processes that ask, Where are we going? How do we get there? How do we measure and control progress? These questions are fine in themselves but they do not go far enough in a world of values-based capitalism.

The central question for executives and companies in this new approach is, What do you stand for? By articulating an answer and driving the systems and processes from the answer, companies can respond quickly to the challenges they face. In the following discussion we show, first, how many companies have dealt with this question, we call it enterprise strategy, to give a sense of the entire enterprise's acting on its values.[8] Second, we show how this framework can easily accommodate environmental questions and green values, taking an example that is not from the environmental area. Most companies have come to environmentalism only lately, and enterprise strategy strikes at the heart of a company and its history. We'll see in the next chapter some examples of companies whose sole purpose, enterprise strategy, is environmentalism. But here we want to leave room for many diverse shades of green, with environmentalism at the periphery as well as at the core of what companies do.

Enterprise Strategy

Scientists at Merck, a pharmaceutical company famous for its discovery of new drugs, thought that they recognized a substance that possibly could be used to cure a dreaded disease: river blindness.[9] River blindness is caused by a parasite that enters the skin when a certain fly bites. The parasites cause itching and eventually make their way to the eyes and cause blindness. River blindness only exists in very isolated parts of the world in which people are very poor and live in the bush. In some villages the disease is so prevalent that blindness is accepted as a normal part of growing old. Needless to say, the people at risk of contracting this disease have no money to buy an expensive, Western-developed drug and have little or no access to Western-style health care. Over 80 million people live in areas in which river blindness is prevalent and yet "the market" for such a drug would have to be funded by outside sources.

Despite the lack of a traditional market Merck decided to go ahead and try to develop a drug to cure river blindness. They did this in part because of their answer to the question of enterprise strategy: What does Merck stand for? George Merck explained that "we try never to forget that medicine is for the people, it is not for the profits. The profits follow, and if we have remembered that, they have never failed to appear. The better we have remembered it, the larger they have been."

Whatever answer is supplied to the question "what do you stand for," it must be formulated in terms of *some values*. An answer in the form of a traditional mission statement that delineates the arenas of action does not go far enough. A vision or other catchy slogan can be too brief. Indeed, many companies see vision/mission/values as going together. It is important to realize that the words of enterprise strategy, in whatever form, are not enough. The answer to the "what do you stand for" question must permeate the company and must provide the ultimate trump card and raison d'être for company action.

Enterprise Strategy and Business Success

Many have argued that businesses are successful because they manage to create and sustain competitive advantage. That is, they have certain capabilities that yield advantages over competitors that are not easily replicated. Competitive advantage is often seen in terms of lower costs, differentiated products, or a focus on a particular part of an industry.

There is a great deal of debate on exactly what processes lead to competitive advantage. C. K. Prahalad and Gary Hamel in *Competing for the Future* have recently suggested that success is not a matter of attaining a "fit" between what a company knows how to do and what the marketplace requires. "Strategy as fit" yields ordinary returns and a complacency that is incompatible with the paradoxes of business.

More interesting is the idea that a company's strategic intent and its core competencies are the sources of competitive advantage. They define a company's aspirations as the kind of company that it wants to be. And they suggest that creating a gap between employees' aspirations and the resources that are available is the engine of creation that drives companies to superior performance.

Managers have to figure out how to meet stretch targets and how to leverage resources, requiring new thinking and innovation instead of searching for new niches. Both the traditional models of strategic fit and the newer ones of core competencies agree that innovation is ultimately the engine of competitive advantage. One sees innovation as a way of equilibrating company and outside forces, whereas the other sees innovation as part and parcel of intent and competency.

We want to suggest that enterprise strategy is one reason companies respond to some changes and not to others, see a need to develop core competencies or not, and pay attention (or not) to external signals. Enterprise strategy, with its reliance on purpose, vision, or values, serves as a source of innovation and core competency and as a renewable resource.

In their groundbreaking book *Built to Last*, Jim Collins and Jerry Porras have identified companies that have sustained superior financial performance over a period of fifty years or longer. One of the reasons for such performance is the realization of a set of values, core ideology, or enterprise strategy (in our terms) that has endured over time. Collins and Porras argue that in addition to Merck companies as diverse as Boeing, Motorola, and Wal-Mart have these core values and that they don't change very much over time.

At Boeing, the "what do you stand for" question is answered by "being pioneers in the field of aeronautics," "tackling huge challenges and risks" such as the Boeing 747 aircraft, in essence, to "eat, breathe and sleep the world of aeronautics."[10] At Motorola, "the company exists to honorably serve the community by providing products and services of superior quality at a fair price" through "continuous self-renewal" and "treating all employees with dignity." At Wal-Mart, "we exist to provide value to our customers—to make their lives better via lower prices and greater selection; all else is secondary." Each company's answer pervades all parts of the company and is shared by all employees. Thus enterprise strategy provides a powerful edifice for innovation and offers the opportunity for adding environmental values to this innovation engine. The process works something like this.

Suppose that we are Merck scientists and we believe in the words of George Merck. We see Merck investing in a cure for river blindness and then giving away the drug in an attempt to wipe out the disease. We are inspired (not just "motivated") to put more energy into creating more new drugs, to create more new competencies or to take advantage of competencies that already exist. Obviously, Merck can't give away all of its drugs and its people know that, which increases their commitment to help Merck survive. Survival is seen in the *moral* and *ethical* answer to the "what do we stand for" question. Companies like Merck may seem fanatical to outsiders because their people approach their work with passion. It is important to them in the same sense in which they value their families.

An outside signal that reaches a company like Merck can activate Merck's values, and then innovation and creativity take over. If innovation is the source of competitive advantage, as Michael Porter and other strategists suggest, then enterprise strategy is the wellspring of innovation. Why bother to innovate? Because something important is at stake—shared values that are worth acting for. Where values are authentic and shared, sustainable competitive advantage emerges. Merck, 3M, J&J, and others are successful precisely because their employees, from the executive suite to the shop floor, believe in the importance of the values. Conversation about those values is lively enough to yield innovation where change is required.

There is no difference in regard to environmental issues. The 3M enterprise strategy is based on three core values: "customer satisfaction, return for investors and being a company employees can be proud to be a part of."[11] Since its inception it has spelled out these values through a focus on innovation, new products, and individual initiative. Building on this enterprise strategy, which 3M has held since its creation, the company adopted a far-reaching environmental policy as early as 1975. The policy states that 3M is committed to solving its own environmental problems, preventing pollution at its source, and developing products that have minimal environmental effects. Ultimately, the company added a fourth value to its core: "respecting our social and physical environment," which it interprets as moving to the idea of sustainability. Sustainability at 3M means "meeting the needs of customers today while respecting the ability of future generations to meet their needs."

Also in 1975, 3M took the unprecedented step of creating a program called Pollution Prevention Pays. This program encouraged employees to discover or create ways to prevent pollution, both in products and processes. Employees discovered ways to turn waste streams into products and to redesign equipment to run more efficiently and to reduce waste at the same time. Since its inception this program has prevented over 750,000 tons of pollutants from entering the biosphere and has saved nearly $1 billion. 3M's ultimate goal is sustainable development, and it is relying on employee innovation to reach that goal. It has invented new products such as the world's first CFC-free, metered dose inhaler for asthma patients and an abrasive to polish everything from surgical instruments to jet engines that does not contribute to air emissions.

It is easy to see that a concern with the environment fits naturally with 3M's overall enterprise strategy. Without a culture of innovation and a focus on new product development, Pollution Prevention Pays would have been empty corporate rhetoric. By building on its core purpose, any company can, with a great deal of work, craft an environmental program to enhance its enterprise strategy.

Creating and Sustaining Enterprise Strategy

Many companies have an enterprise strategy; and the great companies have had one since their founding. Yet many do not. Unless we understand the underlying processes of creating and sustaining enterprise strategy, we will not be able to say much about adding environmental values. Our reading of the business literature and our work with companies over the last twenty years have indicated that the process of creating and sustaining enterprise strategy is complicated by a number of factors.

First, the top people must be committed. Their commitment involves being a role model as well as leading the challenges to the current systems and processes. Second, enterprise strategy cannot be the program of the month. It has to provide some foundations, a common language, and a driving, inspirational force to the key business processes of the company. Third, enterprise strategy must include a provision for challenging the established order. In the years prior to the Tylenol poisoning J&J CEO James Burke sat with thousands of managers worldwide and engaged in challenge meetings in which the Credo was questioned and current systems and practices were laid against the Credo. Fourth, enterprise strategy must be widely participative, not just a management phenomenon. People on the shop floor, people on the firing line with customers, secretaries, and others do the real work of any company. If they don't have a reason for coming to work that is more uplifting than collecting a paycheck, then performance will struggle toward average. Finally, the conversation around enterprise strategy must be alive and ongoing. Too many strategic planning and mission programs are static and routine. Enterprise strategy works when it touches employees deeply, calling on them to sign up for the values that it displays. Only by creating an ongoing shared understanding and not a rigid set of guidelines and rules will enterprise strategy continue to be a clarion call.

In an age of layoffs and restructuring and reengineering, all of this must be done with complete candor and openness. Cynicism is everywhere, and the only way to overcome it is through action. Since no company is perfect and since there will always be mistakes, large doses of humility and good humor are equally in order. Most important, the process of creating and sustaining enterprise strategy must be holographic: It must use the enterprise strategy in its creation. If respect is a value, then all aspects of the process must be respectful. These guidelines are no magic for successfully crafting and implementing enterprise strategy, but in our experience they are the bare minimum for success.

Building a Green Framework for Business Strategy: Principles and Green Values

How does the new logic of business and capitalism, the logic of values, relate to the environment? In the old model competitive advantage was seen as coming from process and technological capabilities, and thus there was little driving force to take on anything "unrelated." Making a process more environmentally friendly could only be seen as coming at the expense of shareholders. Only regulatory threat motivated companies to minimally "green" their strategic framework. But we are arguing for another possibility. If we understand capitalism as a system of cooperation among stakeholders around important values, and if we understand business as being driven by enterprise strategy, then there are no limits to the greening of enterprise strategy. Indeed in chapter 3 we suggest four main ways in which enterprise strategy can adopt "shades of green."

Three Principles

Three core principles are important in greening our new framework for capitalism. What is an obvious environmental truth to some is patently false to others. Rather than embrace either relativism and cynicism or environmental truth, we suggest that we can agree on three fundamental principles: (1) the principle of effects, which states that all of our actions have some environmental effects, and the effects of our actions of the environment can be both global and local; (2) the pinciple of connectedness, which states that human life is biologically dependent on other forms of life and on ecosystems as a whole, including the nonliving aspects of ecosystems; and (3) the principle of responsibility, which states that human beings have a moral responsibility for the effects of their actions.

These three simple, seemingly uncontroversial principles go a long way toward helping us understand the scope of environmental problems. The principle of effects acknowledges that human beings can affect the environment in important ways and that seemingly harmless actions may well have major consequences when those actions are repeated by many over a long period of time.

The second principle, the principle of connectedness, simply says that our fate is inextricably tied to the fate of other species. Although that seems true enough today, not long ago human beings eradicated species without considering the effects of that eradication on human population. Connectedness does not by itself argue for species preservation, but it creates a prima facie duty to examine whether or not a particular species is crucial to maintaining a particular ecosystem. Many environmental debates revolve around what the tradeoff is between, for example, timber and spotted owls. But the real question, as the principle of connectedness implies, is, What is the nature of the relationship between the two and human flourishing? There may well be no tradeoff.

The final principle is the cornerstone of any conversation that is rooted in ethical behavior, namely, human responsibility. Ethics doesn't end with the assumption of responsibility, but it does begin there. The principle of responsibility is what parents in every country and every culture try to teach their children. We teach them to admit the effects of their actions and to take responsibility for them. This principle implies an accountability that is all too often missing on large environmental issues (on all sides of the debate), as it is easy to point fingers, affix blame, and look elsewhere for the solution.

We assume that these three principles are good ones, that you agree with us about their centrality, and that actions which they require will in fact be undertaken. With these principles in mind we want to describe some green values which reinforce these principles.

Declaring Green Values

Our experience and the research on values-driven companies lead us to believe that values, especially green values, must be declared. Values are declared when there is enough conversation about them for the company to state its beliefs. Although statements of values can emerge gradually, at some point, say, a key event, a crisis, or even the questions of cynics, the company must put up or shut up. McDonald's must declare that environment is going to join quality, value, and cleanliness. DuPont must declare zero pollution. 3M must declare that pollution prevention pays. Once values are declared, people will have the courage to try them out— and ultimately to realize them.

These are not idle slogans or public relations strategies. Rather, they are public commitments. To declare a value is to make a commitment to all those within hearing that this value is in force and that it will guide your action.

Declarations of values should be few and far between because the declaration is the easy part. Making the declaration come alive through conflicting systems and processes is the difficult job.

Which green values should we declare? The answer to that question will depend on a host of factors, from the key technologies in an industry to the location of a company's facilities to the employees' answer to our children's future wager.

Some possibilities for green values include (1) "obeying the spirit of environmental laws around the world," (2) zero pollution, (3) using the best available environmental technology, (4) minimizing harm to the environment, (5) avoiding any chances of irreparable harms—the protection principle, (6) protecting the natural environment, and (7) making a commitment to being an environmental leader in the industry.

The logic of values-based capitalism and of enterprise strategy says that whenever green values are declared the organization must be willing to change its processes to align with them. The logic says that the declaration of values must be serious enough to unleash innovation.

Business Strategy and the Innovation Mind-set

In chapter 1 we described five mind-sets, or ways of approaching the environment, that were barriers to the possibilities that we saw with shades of green. Recall that these mind-sets included the regulatory mindset, the cost-benefit mind-set, the constraint mind-set, the sustainable development mind-set, and the greenwashing mind-set. Values-based capitalism in general and enterprise strategy in particular require none of these five frames. Rather, there is another underlying approach that goes well with the ideas we have spelled out in this chapter. For lack of a better term we have dubbed this mind-set the "innovation mind-set."

The innovation mind-set is experimental. Because it is driven by values that are important there is little iconoclastic structure. In the innovation mind-set almost everything is up for grabs. The key values remain Archimedean fixed points about which innovation revolves. The willingness to experiment, to try something different and to fix it, rather than to engage in the perfect planning exercise, is characteristic of this mind-set. It heeds the dictum of pragmatist philosopher John Dewey that the social world is a living experiment. "Let's try it" is heard more often than "yes, but."

The innovation mind-set is relentless. Once again, because it is driven by values and the values are important, there is simply no other alternative. We once observed an organizational member who was an environmentalist and was appalled by her institution's lack of attention to recycling. Every avenue this person took to raise the issue turned out to be a blind alley until she hit upon the idea of doing the recycling herself. Many days she could be seen carrying green sacks of bottles and cans away from the worksite. The sheer determination and relentlessness that she showed in gathering and recycling many pounds of material, finally rubbed off on the organization, and today it has an active recycling program.

Finally, the innovation mind-set is contentious, filled with conflict. Values have a way of inviting questions and conflict. Far from the popular view that values are about "being nice" to everyone, values-based organizations use values to ask hardheaded, tough-minded questions. The values are considered as important in themselves, and so little else is sacred. The innovation mind-set is a willingness to continually ask, Why are we doing it this way? and to invent a better way that better realizes the values.

Conclusions

In this chapter we have sketched a new understanding of business that is based on values. We have suggested that green values are easily consistent with this framework. The resulting values-based capitalism and enterprise strategy are meant to capture the thousands of values-based innovations that are driving our dynamic system of capitalism. Values are not slogans that promote happy talk, feeling good, and being nice to one another. They reflect our deepest concerns and cares. They are what make us human. They must be a part of our understanding of business, indeed they are the core, the wellspring, the drivers of profitability and employee commitment. This chapter has merely sketched how they can be important in business today. There is much more to be said, as the retelling of the story of capitalism will unfold over the next decade. We turn now to methods of incorporating environmental values into the very fabric of business, to shades of green.

CHAPTER THREE

Four Shades of Green

Introduction

McDonald's restaurant chain has long tried to be sensitive to issues that concern its customers. Founder Ray Kroc built McDonald's on the basis of values: quality, service, cleanliness, and value. During the 1980s, McDonald's began several initiatives around the environment but was having little success and was coming under a great deal of criticism for its decisions about the use of polystyrene containers. In 1989 McDonald's and the Environmental Defense Fund devised a joint project to address the problem of solid waste generated by McDonald's franchises, as a way to begin adding "environment" to McDonald's values. Originally the two sides engaged in protracted negotiations to maintain the external validity of the EDF and McDonald's autonomy in making its own decisions. After several working meetings the parties discovered so much in common that these initial concerns were set aside as they worked together to recycle waste and save millions of dollars.[1]

This is but one of many stories that are beginning to be told about how environmental values and business go together. Is there a way to systematically understand how to green business strategy? Zero pollution may not be appropriate for every business, and recycling some materials may not make sense. Every company can't make first-rate consumer products out of recycled plastic à la Patagonia, and energy audits à la the Body Shop may have limited applicability.

Our argument in the preceding chapters can be summarized along the following lines. There are many ways to run successful businesses, many ways to put values into business, and many ways to be green. If we are to turn the odds of an environmental crisis in our favor, it will not be because of a single technological leap forward, such as nuclear fusion. Rather, we believe that the key to success lies in the creative power of capitalism—the power of innovation. We need many businesses differently declaring green values and working to realize them.

We don't need a particular shade of green embedded in government policy, cost-benefit analysis, or even sustainable development. We do need a willingness to experiment, to realize the environmental values that we truly believe. Acting in bad faith does little and the first shade of green, legal green, tries to prevent such action.

We have identified four broad ways to incorporate environmental values into business strategy—four shades of green. Each shade requires the innovation mind-set. It is one thing to say that the creative power of capitalism can be harnessed to make the earth a greener place, yet it is quite another to actually do it. Each shade of green rests on certain values, some resting primarily on the role of citizenship and others depending on a view of respect for the earth itself. In this chapter we lay out each shade and suggest how it can lead to competitive advantage and business success. We also say a little about the underlying capabilities and processes that must be put in place if a particular shade of green is to be realized. But first there is a caveat.

The shades of green are not mutually exclusive. Even dark green companies will see the need to obey the law. You may think of the shades as stages of development with the idea that the more a company begins to address environmental concerns the darker green it will become. But we caution you against this interpretation, for we believe that green values are complex, especially when they interact with other business values such as respect for the individual, customer service, quality, and the like. We are less interested in seeing a particular environmental value narrowly adopted than in seeing a panoply of some environmental values broadly adopted.

You can think of these shades of green as strategic postures—generalized approaches that more or less describe a company's environmental attitude. They are the "top of mind" approaches that companies take when faced with an environmental challenge. As such, they are connected to the mission and vision of the business. A company whose primary mission is serving stockholders is more likely to adopt a light or legal green shade. A company whose mission is to provide unparalleled customer service will gravitate toward market green. If the company's vision is to balance the interests of suppliers, employees, shareholders, communities, and so on, then stakeholder green will rule the day. Finally, a company that sees itself as bound up with the ecosystem and its health will prefer a dark green.

Light Green or Legal Green

A company can craft competitive advantage simply by paying attention to the law or its interpretations in regulations or judicial decisions.

Better, Faster, Cheaper

First of all, companies can use the law to enhance the innovation mind-set among their employees. Suppose that a particular regulation has been announced that limits the amount of a gas that can be emitted. One approach would be for every company in the industry to adopt the same technology in its production process to comply with the regulation. Everyone would incur the same costs, and no one would be at a disadvantage because of the regulation. Yet another approach would be for a company to figure out a better way to eliminate the gas, perhaps changing its production process, its product mix, the content of the waste stream, and so on. You get the idea: Regulation can serve as an impetus for innovation. The company that figures out how to comply with the regulation better, faster, and cheaper will have a competitive advantage.

A second way to craft sustainable competitive advantage from regulation is to figure out how to make the regulation irrelevant. Can the production process be changed to do without the substance covered by the regulation? Often the very search for alternatives is the source of new and unexpectedly good results. Searching to comply with dioxin emission regulation led Union Camp to invent a process that was virtually dioxin free, which was the envy of the industry.[2]

Firms in the steel industry had a variety of options for responding to the Clean Air Act Amendments of 1990 with respect to the production of coke. The options ranged from piecemeal fixes of old facilities to trying to meet the requirements of the law, to investing in new technology to make iron without coke. Clearly, a firm that made a breakthrough in direct iron making would have a competitive advantage as countries around the world began to clean up dirty industries such as coke production.

Influencing the Regulatory Process

Yet another strategy for crafting competitive advantage through law is to take a proactive stance to influence the very nature of the law. Companies often make clumsy attempts at this, especially in the environmental area. The early history of environmentalism in the United States is primarily one of companies seeking to influence the regulatory process by opposing environmental legislation and regulation or, if pushed, seeking to make it more favorable to their industry. Such a strategy does little for innovation and is ultimately not sustainable.

The Spirit and the Letter of the Law

Each of these light or legal green strategies rests on the light green or legal green principle: *Create and sustain competitive advantage by ensuring that your company is in compliance with the law.*

We are not arguing that there is always competitive advantage in obeying the law and complying with regulations. Rather, it is possible to craft such advantage through the innovation mindset. Too often, however, the cost-benefit mind-set takes over. The latest environmental regulation is immediately decried as being bad for business, costing jobs, and putting the company at a competitive disadvantage on the international battlefield of business. Usually, merely complying with the letter of the law is not sufficient. Companies that find competitive advantage in regulation are the ones that try to find a better way to fulfill the spirit of the law. In short, they are beginning to adopt some environmental values.

Light Green Values and Processes

What environmental values underlie a light green environmental strategic posture? The obvious candidates are respect for law and good citizenship. There is simply no way to enforce environmental regulations across the board. It would take too many inspections, the costs would be too great, and the results would not be guaranteed. The approach to environmental regulation has always been to rely on voluntary compliance to a large degree. This is not to say that there have not been harsh enforcement mechanisms, or control systems to catch violators, but if you think about the scope of business and industry, environmental law works in a similar fashion to other areas of the law. By and large, most people want to obey the law and will go to a fair amount of trouble to do so.

The value of being a good citizen also undergirds the light green environmental posture. Even the company that espouses only the maximization of shareholder value knows that being seen as a good citizen in the community has positive value. In large part environmental law exists because we have not demanded that each of us take account of our effects on the environment. We have not demanded that good citizenship include responsibility to the ecosystem. This is true for business executives and community members. We are trying to make our political process do the work of our conceptual apparatus and the results are mixed. If we had the mind-set that being a good citizen included conserving the earth for those who follow, then, voluntarily and as a matter of course, we would do many of the things that environmental law requires. We shall return to this point in chapter 5 when we consider how to craft better conversations for society as a whole.

41

A company that values respect for the law and good citizenship must put processes in place that make its actions consistent with those values. If a light green environmental posture is to lead to truly sustainable competitive advantage, then organizational processes must support it. Attention must be paid to interpreting the law, from regulation to judicial decision, and that attention must come from the entire organization, from the legal and public affairs department down to the shop floor, where real innovation takes place. There must be an explicit strategy for citizenship, through public relations, community involvement, or other systems. The following checklist of questions can be used to assess whether or not light or legal green is sustainable:

1. Are managers and other employees aware of major environmental legislation that affects our company?
2. Is our company in compliance with the law? Is any outstanding environmental litigation under way?
3. What are the proposed environmental regulations, legislative initiatives, or judicial opinions that affect our business? Are we aware of these issues on a global basis? Do our plant managers and product specialists routinely consider how environmental regulations affect their area of responsibility?
4. Is there a process for employees to come forward and suggest ideas that can circumvent legislation/regulation? Alternatively, is there a process for blowing the whistle where we are willfully not compliant with the law?
5. Does our business strategy process routinely assess the environmental impact of our operations within the context of the regulatory process?
6. Do our corporate contributions/citizenship initiatives reflect a concern with environmental legislation/regulation?
7. How well are we positioned to take advantage of new regulatory initiatives vis à vis our competitors?

It has often been suggested that innovation does not readily follow environmental legislation—that we are being too optimistic about what is possible in this arena. We have several responses. The first is that sometimes the regulations that are proposed simply make no environmental sense. There is too much disagreement in the political process to craft law that admits of innovative ways of fulfilling its spirit. We believe that the regulatory lessons of past decades have largely been learned and that we are moving toward regulatory schemes that are more output oriented, with the means being left up to businesses. But there are stupid regulations and we have no answer for that. We insist that we not base our entire view of what is possible in business on the fact that sometimes environmental regulation makes no sense. Second, what we have suggested here is far from easy. It requires an intense and authentic effort to be a part of the public policy process. Half-hearted attempts to throw up roadblocks or rewrite rules and laws are not what we have in mind. We have suggested that a company which makes an all-out effort using the innovation mind-set can craft competitive advantage through a posture of legal green.

Aren't companies that adopt legal green at a disadvantage in host countries whose home companies do not have to abide by the same laws? Perhaps, but evidence is beginning to mount that the process of innovation is so central to business that operating in countries with strict environmental laws makes a company more competitive elsewhere in the world, not less competitive.[3] There are thorny issues of both ethics and cultural relativism when companies operate across borders. No area of business is exempt from these issues, and environmentalism simply brings them to the forefront.

Market Green

There are even more ways to craft competitive advantage in a company by paying attention to customer preferences. Citizens who become more conscious of environmental issues alter their preferences as consumers. More so today than at any other time in history, we see environmental attributes becoming an important part of buying decisions, and this is happening at the consumer and business-to-business levels.

Responding to Customer Desires

In trying to decide how to package its Lenoir fabric softener in Germany, Procter and Gamble had to balance a number of product variables, including cost, ease of use, ability to gain shelf space, and effects on the environment. As is almost always the case, the environmental effects were not easy to discern. Excess packaging has one effect, but the recyclability of the package, the effects of the product on the water supply, and the amount of energy used may point to different ones. Procter and Gamble tried to gauge what its customers wanted and responded with a refillable container, with the refills being sold in a bulk package.[4]

The Nature Company, Natural Wonder, the Rainforest Cafe, and others have developed retail stores to respond to environmental consumer preferences. Natural Wonder and others donate a portion of their proceeds to environmental organizations. These retail outlets have attempted to forge competitive advantage by offering environmental products and services that customers want.[5]

Supermarkets in the United States have responded to consumer preferences for ease of recycling by making their plastic bags recyclable at the stores. Recycling has changed the dynamics of the pulp and paper industry. The increase in the recycling of newspaper has led to the construction of new de-inking facilities and has reduced the need for virgin-timber production facilities.

Although responding to consumer preferences leads to a lot of environmental activity, it does not necessarily lead to a better, cleaner world. The first problem is greenwashing, which we discussed in chapter 1—making merely cosmetic changes and engaging in green talk. But, a more severe problem is related. Often consumer preferences are a function of fashion and style or the latest environmental news. As we have stated repeatedly, the only facts are that there are no sure fast facts. So, just responding to customer preferences may well not go far enough.

Being Proactive: Leading Consumer Preferences

Great companies often shape customer preferences, not in a manipulative sense but from the collaborative point of view. Companies work with their customers in order to better understand and define their needs. Electric utilities such as New England Electric System have been leaders in helping customers understand the environmental impact of their energy use and have used a variety of programs to help their customers live in a more environmentally friendly way. New England Electric recently received an environmental award from the Massachusetts Audubon Society for its work in helping its customers be more conservation oriented.[6]

Xerox's Design for the Environment program is aimed at building environmental attributes into the product design process. Such a program has to be closely tied to feedback from customers. In addition its Waste-Free Office program helps Xerox customers eliminate waste in their corporate offices. Xerox sees this effort as a way to lead customers into a more environmentally safe future. Spokesman Jack Agar says, "We're going to have a major focus on environmental marketing. . . . I think we can show that the way Xerox is going to manage documents in the future is very environmentally responsible."

The Dell Computer Corporation has worked with its large business and government customers to develop more environmentally friendly computers. Recently it has developed a new chassis for its computers that is recyclable. The project grew out of customer concerns over the disposal of old machines.

By leading consumer preferences instead of just responding to them, companies position themselves to sustain their advantage by finding new markets and new customers. Environmentalism isn't just talk at companies like Xerox and Dell. In fact many such companies take the next step and articulate some principles that guide them in developing environmentally friendly strategies.

Principle-Based Marketing

Environmental issues are tricky. Often the key to making progress is simply believing that environmentalism in whatever form is important and committing to do something. Difficulties like the impact on future generations and unforeseen consequences make responding to or even leading consumer preferences problematic.

A number of companies have tried to crystallize what they believe into a principle about customers. McDonald's has developed the following consumer-oriented policy: "McDonald's believes it has a special responsibility to protect our environment for future generations. This responsibility is derived from our unique relationship with millions of consumers worldwide— whose quality of life tomorrow will be affected by our stewardship of the environment today."

McDonald's has articulated a concern for future generations that is based on a practical business consideration: its relationship with its current customers. This principle has led to productive partnerships with environmental groups and suppliers, as McDonald's has tried to become a leader in its industry.[7]

Green Marketing

Each of these market green strategic postures, responding to customer preference, leading customer preferences, and principle-based marketing rests on the fundamental insight of market green, articulated already in chapter 1: *Create and sustain competitive advantage by paying attention to the environmental preferences of customers.*

Again, we are not arguing that competitive advantage is always found in the market green principle but that it offers opportunity and possibility if approached with an innovation mind-set.

Market Green Values and Processes

What environmental values undergird a strategic posture of market green? There is really only one and that is some notion of ultimate consumer sovereignty. Whatever its theory of why business works, whether its ultimate goal is to serve shareholders with maximum profits or to balance the interest of stakeholders, market green companies must believe in paying attention to customers.

As a business value, "dedication to customers" is hard to argue with, but note that it also has an ethical element. Dedication to customers does not mean "maximizing returns from this single transaction" nor does it involve manipulation of needs or of information. It involves an ethic of service. It involves promising to try to meet the needs of a customer within the reasonable operating expertise of the company. Some companies, like Hewlett Packard, Nordstrom, and Motorola, live this value every day. Others, such as the stereotypical used car dealer, obviously do not. Market green can avoid greenwash and green talk when dedication to customer is a lived value rather than merely a spoken one. If dedication to customers is to be a lived value, then processes must be in place that tie it to all of a company's operations. There is nothing special about the environmental attributes of a product or service. It is just one part of doing the total customer service job. The following checklist can be used to see whether market green is sustainable in a company.

1. Do employees have regular conversations with customers about their environmental issues and concerns?
2. Do employees routinely benchmark best environmental practices in the industry? Across other related industries?
3. Does the company know the environmental impact of customers' behavior with its product?
4. Does the company know the environmental strategy (shade of green) of the customer? (Assuming the customer is another business.)
5. Does the business strategy process regularly take account of customers' environmental issues?
6. Does the new product development and design process take environmental issues into account? Is it in touch with customers' needs?
7. Is there regular and candid feedback on company perfor-

mance with customers? Does this feedback include environmental issues?

8. Do decision makers have something at stake such as rewards for how well the company is dedicated to serving customers? Are there direct, tangible, customer-driven measurements?

The road to dedication to customers is a long one. Bureaucratic processes that have become entrenched over time and add no value to customers are sometimes hard to spot. The recent trend of restructuring or reengineering has been largely an exercise in putting customer-responsive processes in place despite organizational structure, and changing the culture of a company via these new processes. It is no surprise that many of these reengineering processes have focused on environmentally friendly ideas such as recycling of waste, conservation, and streamlined and more automated processes.

Market green sees business as a cooperative deal between the company and its customers. In the international world of modern business this offers a large challenge to companies large and small. Dedication to customers as a value helps to focus attention on sustaining competitive advantage.

Stakeholder Green

More and more companies are coming to realize that business success can only be sustained by taking stakeholder interests into account in all business processes. This statement is not as revolutionary as it may seem simply because it is easy to acknowledge that the interests of customers, suppliers, employees, and financiers have to be aligned over time. In a relatively free and open society, the community's interest must also be aligned or it will use the political process to force such an alignment through legislation and regulation. The history of the rise of the regulation of business and markets is precisely the history of companies and executives who continually act against the interests of communities where their operations are located and where their employees and customers live.

Taking a stakeholder approach offers even more sources of

competitive advantage than market and legal green. We can begin by sorting out several senses of "stakeholder," each of which offers different hues of stakeholder green. The first sense, the managerial view, is the narrowest, and it says that customers, employees, suppliers, and community have a means-oriented stake in the achievement of shareholder or financier value. The second sense, the values-based view, is that each group in addition to financiers has a legitimate interest in the firm. Indeed companies are just the collaborative ventures of stakeholders over time. The third sense, the political view, says that interest groups such as media, NGOs, government agencies, and others are stakeholders who must be taken into account for either managerial or values-based reasons. Regardless of what we think about stakeholders, there are many ways to craft competitive advantage.

Linking Stakeholder Relationships

Great companies are, for the most part, oriented toward stakeholders. They craft competitive advantage through linking stakeholder relationships in unique ways that create value for each stakeholder and engender superior financial returns. The logic is simple. In his groundbreaking work over the last fifteen years, management guru Tom Peters has identified story after story of how managers have put together the interests of suppliers, employees, and customers. More recently Poras and Collins tell the stories of companies that are "built to last," and here too we find case after case of how a concern with the overarching purpose of businesses from Merck to GE has led to forging together the interests of multiple stakeholders.

Creating these partnerships or collaborations is a natural extension of market green, and in this sense stakeholder green is a logical "spelling out" of market green. Responding to customers' environmental preferences often requires paying environmental attention to suppliers and employees, and that often leads to a concern with community. For example, Earth's Best is an organic baby food company that insists on 0 percent detectable levels of pesticide residues on its products. If Earth's Best is responding to a market preference for organic baby food, it is easy to see how it simply must be concerned with suppliers. In fact the company is extremely particular in its choice of organic farms, insisting that the farm has used organic practices for a minimum of three years. Additionally, Earth's Best involves its employees in forging the supplier-customer link by sending them to inspect farms, test for pesticide levels, and observe how produce is processed and packaged, to assure that no unnecessary or unnatural steps are taken.

British Petroleum has begun to publish an environmental annual report so that key stakeholders will have information on what the company is doing in the environmental area and on what work remains to be done.[8] Their goals are simply "no accidents, no harm to people, and no damage to the environment." By committing to publishing the results of their efforts to measure progress on these goals, BP has made a public declaration of the importance of the environment to its stakeholder constituencies.

Whole Foods Market is the largest retailer of natural foods in the United States and owns stores throughout the country including Bread and Circus, Mrs. Gooch's Natural Foods, and Fresh Fields. Their emphasis has been on providing food and natural products that are harmless (either a natural product or one that has proven harmless through time) and have been tested without the use of animals. Foods and products, such as makeup and shampoo, free of artificial flavors, colors, sweeteners, and synthetic preservatives are promoted, as are organically grown foods. Seafood, meat, and poultry contain no added hormones, stimulants, antibiotics, or sodium nitrate. The bakery uses grain that has not been bleached or bromated. Information used to help educate the consumer on abusive animal testing practices is distributed in the stores, as well as information on a variety of environmental issues. It is easy to see that managing such an enterprise must pay special attention to the supplier-employee-customer link, and Whole Foods has gone even further, involving itself in local communities. It plans to open stores in low income neighborhoods in an effort to put "a free-range chicken in every pot."

Even the U.S. Postal Service is getting into the act. It recently undertook a comprehensive program of operational efficiency, education of employees and customers, and other recycling programs aimed at eliminating the impact of mail on landfills. This is an instance of following the logic of the business, in this case mail, to examine the relationship with communities, or at least one aspect of that relationship.

Beyond Compliance to Voluntarism

Stakeholder green requires companies to take an active approach to understanding stakeholders and their concerns. Instead of focusing exclusively on complying with legal or regulatory rules, a stakeholder approach relies on a philosophy of voluntarism—that business is in fact a citizen of its many communities and should be involved in issues of concern to them. Nowhere is this more true than in those industries that have been accused in the past of being very heavy polluters, such as chemicals and oil. Voluntarism often means a competitive advantage well ahead of any regulatory regime that forces change.

The chemical industry has begun to be much more responsive to community concerns via a program called Responsible Care. Literally hundreds of community panels have been formed to offer advice and input into company decisions that affect local communities. Dow Chemical selects twenty diverse people and meets with them monthly, a facilitator with the panel setting the agenda.[9]

DuPont, long considered the rogue of the environmental movement, has spent a great deal of time and effort trying to incorporate more green thinking into its corporate philosophy and has explicitly relied on the stakeholder idea to do so: "We affirm to all our stakeholders, including our employees, customers, shareholders, and the public, that we will conduct our business with respect and care for the environment. We will implement those strategies that build successful businesses and achieve the greatest benefit for all our stakeholders without compromising the ability of future generations to meet their needs." This principle puts "stakeholder green" in the light of all of the obligations that a company may have to its stakeholders, only some of which are environmental obligations. By fitting stakeholder green into a broader stakeholder philosophy, executives will be better positioned to see tradeoffs and to go beyond the simplistic "economic versus environmental" arguments that are so tiresome.[10]

Shell Oil, in response to a spill at the Martinez refinery in California, began a community advisory panel to develop greater responsiveness to the concerns of the local area. The panel has had an impact on such diverse areas as the operating of the refinery and the channeling of corporate philanthropy into the local community. A study by Cohen, Chess, Lynn, and Busenberg concludes that one of the key elements in the building of trust between Shell and its community was Shell's offer to pay for independent technical assistance for the panel.[11]

Negotiating with Stakeholders

Companies that take an active approach toward their stakeholders by forming community panels and so on have to be prepared to negotiate rather than just persuade the community to accept the company's position. Negotiating with stakeholders on environmental issues is very tricky for many of the reasons that we have outlined in earlier chapters; namely, that environmentalists and businesspeople do not often share worldviews or vocabularies and often do not trust each other's point of view. In chapter 1 we examined an issue of stakeholder negotiation with a good outcome. Recall the McDonald's–Environmental Defense Fund story. McDonald's crafted part of a competitive advantage by being better equipped to work with and negotiate with key environmental stakeholders. However, in the real world there are not always happy endings.

One of the more celebrated recent cases of stakeholder green implemented through negotiation was a decision by Conoco to invest in Ecuador.[12] Conoco engaged its stakeholders in an elaborate process that resulted in an agreement to proceed with rainforest oil development in a manner acceptable to most of the stakeholders. However, the process was far from problem free. There were many environmental groups from both Ecuador and the United States, as well as groups representing the native peoples of Ecuador, the Haorani. Add in the government ministries, and it was often unclear just who was speaking for whom. Finally after more than a year of negotiating Conoco gave up and withdrew from Ecuador, stating that it couldn't reach an agreement that was acceptable to all stakeholders that was financially viable as well. Being willing to negotiate is a necessary but not sufficient condition. And sometimes agreements that get the approval of multiple parties are too broad to be implementable.

Stakeholder Green

Each of these methods of crafting competitive advantage—by linking stakeholder relationships, shifting from compliance to voluntarism, and negotiating with stakeholders—is in the spirit of the following principle: *Create and sustain competitive advantage by responding to the environmental preferences of stakeholders.*

We are not arguing that competitive advantage can always be found by paying attention to stakeholder preferences but that it can be and often is. Stakeholder preferences can even conflict within a particular group. However, behind every stakeholder concern is a potential marketplace, if approached with the innovation mind-set.

Stakeholder Green Values and Processes

What environmental values provide the foundations for a stakeholder shade of green? It is easy to see that the values which provide impetus for both legal green and market green also support stakeholder green. After all, respect for law and good citizenship are part and parcel of a company's relationship with its community, and the customer is an important stakeholder. But we need to go further.

Unless a company and its executives really value cooperation and collaboration, a stakeholder approach will not work. In order to forge a deal that is sustainable over a long period of time, conflicting stakeholder interests must be negotiated and there must be continuous renewal to the stakeholder relationships themselves.

Novo Nordisk invited in outside stakeholders and opened its business for the advice and criticism of stakeholders on environmental issues. By invoking a process of actively seeking advice from stakeholders, the company is in a better position to design value creation processes that truly meet joint needs. Novo Nordisk has developed the reputation of being committed to implementing sustainable development through paying attention to its stakeholders.[13] The following checklist includes questions for designing processes that help a company become stakeholder green.

1. Does everyone in the organization understand our mission to serve stakeholders? Are we committed to being a great company?
2. Is there a well-understood process for disagreement or dissent if it happens that we are not living up to our mission?
3. Do we routinely see how stakeholder interests converge? Does our business strategy process encourage cross-stakeholder thinking?
4. Are we constantly trying to create employee-supplier-customer linkages?
5. Do we have explicit strategies for our communities? Are we attuned to the least advantaged members of the community?
6. Are we candid with ourselves when stakeholder interests conflict? Are we candid with our stakeholders?
7. Do we have the innovation mind-set—a willingness to try new ideas and strategies to serve stakeholders?
8. Is it difficult to distinguish organizational members from stakeholders?

Ernst Winter and Sohn has manufactured diamond tools since the mid-1980s. It has implemented within the structure of the business an "integrated system of environmentalist business management," which deals with all environmental concerns of the company from training employees to recycling programs to the management of materials. The business is likened conceptually to a living organism, with each employee being a cell in the corporate organism. Employees are educated about environmental concerns and issues through seminars and lectures. In 1985, an eighteen-month pilot program included sending environmental experts to the households of many employees to help them evaluate how negative environmental impacts can be reduced in the home. Several other German businesses and nonprofit organizations subsequently followed suit. Winter installed an environmental manager who conducts the environmental programs within the company. It has created a diamond blade stone cutter that has greatly reduced the noise pollution, eliminated asbestos, and decreased hazardous dust. It has converted three of its manufacturing plants from oil to natural gas, which is more efficient. It encourages other companies to insist on low pollution and the development of alternative products. Additionally, the company provides financial support to several conservation organizations in Germany.

Is the Environment a Stakeholder?

Value creation is the province of all stakeholders in a collaborative deal. No one stakeholder is asked to forego value over time, though there may be cases of winners and losers in the short term. If one stakeholder group always loses, then this is tantamount to not taking their claims seriously.

The Tom's of Maine company has redesigned the company around a dual concern for the environment and its employees. It has built its business on all-natural, environmentally friendly toothpaste and deodorant. It has given over $100,000 per year to the Rainforest Alliance and supports curbside recycling in its Maine environment. It refuses to animal test its products and uses environmentally friendly packaging materials. And it is very competitive, moving from a specialty niche in health food stores to national grocery chains. Tom Chappell has stated, "You can be a hard-assed competitor and still run a business with soul."[14] The value creation process at Tom's pulls together the interests of stakeholders and the interests of employees, and it asks a tough question: Should we include the environment as a stakeholder?

Dark Green

Architect and philosopher William McDonough often tells the story of a person who wants to go from Charlottesville to Atlanta but finds herself speeding along at a hundred miles per hour toward Washington in the opposite direction. McDonough argues that slowing down to forty-five miles per hour won't fix the problem. Rather the driver needs to stop what she is doing and turn around.

Advocates of dark green values might argue that legal, market, and stakeholder green are too little too late. They suggest that we need to rethink business in a particular shade of green, one that is sustainable.

Sustainable Business and Deep Ecology

Seeking competitive advantage through making a company sustainable is a fast-growing segment of green businesses. Companies as different as Monsanto and Patagonia are trying to figure out how to rethink commerce in a way that is consistent with principles of deep ecology. Deep ecology is the view that says that we should "go lightly" in our footprint on the earth, that we shouldn't do any harm, and that we should reuse and even put back resources that we take from the earth. Some deep ecologists eschew business of any kind, but there are a number who have latched onto the concept of sustainability to search for a darker shade of green for capitalism. IKEA is a good example of work going on in this area.

IKEA, a Sweden-based furniture retailer, has taken dark green values seriously. It has adopted the philosophy known as the Natural Step, founded by Karl-Henrik Robert. The Natural Step is based on four key principles: (1) substances from the earth's crust must not systematically increase in nature; (2) substances produced by society must not systematically increase in nature; (3)

physical basis for the productivity and diversity of nature must not be systematically deteriorated; and (4) just and efficient use of energy and other resources. By following the Natural Step, companies attempt to make their operations more sustainable and to "go lightly" in concert with the ideas of deep ecology.

In its attempt to implement these principles in a large worldwide retailer, IKEA adopted the following environmental policy. The company is essentially being reinvented along the lines suggested by the Natural Step and their own philosophy.

IKEA's Environmental Policy[15] Approved by the Board in 1991

At IKEA, we shall always strive to minimize any possible damaging effects to the environment which may result as a consequence of our activities.

We shall therefore always strive to ensure that our product range with regard to raw materials, production, distribution, use and disposal is environmentally friendly.

We shall therefore always strive to ensure that customers purchasing articles from IKEA feel that they are contributing to a better environment through their choice of products. Customers shall therefore be provided with factual information about the characteristics of products, component materials, etc. which they require in order to arrive at a purchasing decision.

We shall therefore strive to ensure that environmentally friendly, preferably recyclable, materials are used. Products and materials, which, according to Group Management's evaluation, have detrimental effects on the environment should if possible be phased out or substituted by environmentally better alternatives.

We shall therefore strive to ensure that all internal activities involving our stores, warehouses, offices, transport, etc. are performed in such a way as to contribute to a better environment. Our staff shall have access to the necessary education and information on current environment questions.

Suggestions for measures beneficial to the environment shall be actively encouraged and adopted.

We shall therefore always strive to ensure that the following activities shall be actively encouraged and supported within our area of operations; research and environmentally kind products, materials and production processes.

We shall furthermore always continue to fulfill our basic principles, namely to maintain a real price advantage for products, which from our customer's point of view are comparable with those of our competitors, and to provide the best possible offer within each function.

Each manager is responsible within his/her area for the planning and implementation of the above policy.

Patagonia and its founder, Yvon Chouinard, are well-known for a commitment to the environment. In 1984 they began a process of setting aside 10 percent of pretax profits that Chouinard called "our earth tax." He believed that this must be done before government required it else the Earth would be unsavable. Chouinard embraced deep ecology but could not figure out how to make such a commitment consistent with a company that promoted consumption. He and the company's senior managers decided to launch an inquiry, an investigation into how to manage the company in a way that would be self-sustaining for the next hundred years. While the jury is still out, Patagonia has decided to stop sending their catalogs by direct mail, to scale back growth, and to promote the use of innovative recyclables to make their products. They make an entire line of fabric and clothing out of recycled soda bottles.[16]

McDonough's Principles

William McDonough thinks that it is time for another industrial revolution, and he believes that it could be as important as the first one. He argues that we must see the creation of dark green businesses as "a design problem." "How do we design businesses that restore the health of the earth and the ecosystem?" is the kind of question that we should be asking. To spur this conversation McDonough has formulated the following Hannover Principles,[17] which he developed for the site of the World's Fair in 2000.

- Insist on rights of humanity and nature to coexist in a healthy, supportive, diverse and sustainable condition.
- Recognize interdependence. The elements of human design interact with and depend upon the natural world, with broad and diverse implications at every scale. Expand design considerations to recognize even distant effects.
- Respect relationships between spirit and matter. Consider all aspects of human settlement including community, dwelling, industry and trade in terms of existing and evolving connections between spiritual and material consciousness.
- Accept responsibility for the consequences of design decisions upon human well-being, the viability of natural systems and their right to coexist.
- Create safe objects of long-term value. Do not burden future generations with requirements for maintenance or vigilant administration of potential danger due to the careless creation of products, processes or standards.
- Eliminate the concept of waste. Evaluate and optimize the full life-cycle of products and processes to approach the state of natural systems, in which there is no waste.
- Rely on natural energy flows. Human designs should, like the living world, derive their creative forces from perpetual solar income. Incorporate this energy efficiently and safely for responsible use.
- Understand the limitations of design. No human creation lasts forever and design does not solve all problems. Those who create and plan should practice humility in the face of nature. Treat nature as a model and mentor, not an inconvenience to be evaded and controlled.
- Seek constant improvement by the sharing of knowledge. Encourage direct and open communication between col-

leagues, patrons, manufacturers, and users to link long-term sustainable considerations with ethical responsibility, and reestablish the integral relationship between processes and human activity.

A number of companies are trying to craft competitive advantage by applying McDonough's principles to their business. Monsanto has taken these principles to heart and has begun to get out of its traditional chemical businesses. Its basic idea is to apply knowledge to the seeds to grow crops, rather than the traditional method of applying chemicals to the soil. Its shift of focus to biotechnology is not without environmental risks and controversy.[18]

A Swiss textile company, Rohner Textile, has used some of these ideas to make fabrics with materials that actually purify the water that enters the mills.[19] The use of natural materials and dyes helps abate the usual problems of wastewater and pollution.

The dark green principle summarizes attempts to apply sustainability or a more thoroughgoing idea like the Hannover Principles: *Create and sustain value in a way that sustains and cares for the Earth.*

Dark Green Values and Processes

A commitment to dark green is no small matter. More than other shades of green, the company that strives to be dark green needs to have a clear idea of its purpose and must have extraordinary knowledge of the effects of its business on the environment. Its commitment may well transcend the bounds of the company and even its stakeholders as it tries to create a different world.

For example, the Real Goods Trading Corporation has incorporated the idea of sustainability into its mission statement to give it impetus to develop products that do no harm to the environment: "Real Goods is in business to provide the knowledge and products to redirect the world toward a sustainable future where all living things are recognized as interconnected. Our merchandise provides tools . . . that are free of extractive, exploitative, and environmental abuse throughout their life cycle. . . . We will strive to educate through our products, our communications, and our example, that a simple, self-reliant lifestyle is the best way of sustaining the planet's limited resources for future generations."[20]

Agra Quest in Davis, California, has developed and marketed environmentally friendly natural pesticides. Natural substances produced by microbes and plants are used to kill pests as effectively as chemical pesticides, and they are resilient against excessive heat, rain, or sunlight. Their mission is big: "To redefine the crop industry by continually introducing innovative and environmentally responsible products and services."[21]

The following dark green checklist includes questions for beginning the process of developing a dark green strategy.

1. Does everyone in the organization understand our environmental values? Are we all really committed to them? Enough to try changing the world?
2. Have we built in processes which ensure that we will continuously question whether or not we are living our values?
3. Do we have a clear idea of the design problem that we are trying to solve?
4. Is it possible to create a supportive business ecosystem of powerful partners, suppliers, customers, and complementers who share our commitment to environmental values?
5. What is our strategy for potential growth or retrenchment? Could we greatly expand or shrink and be true to our values?
6. Do we have the innovation mind-set—a willingness to try new ideas and strategies to realize our values?

Philosophical Questions and Business Strategy

Once we raise the issue of whether or not a business can be dark green we face a thicket of thorny philosophical issues. What is our underlying view of how humans should live? What are the basic values that bind us together and tear us apart? Are there different views of the world in terms of how the human-environment relationship should evolve? How are we to understand environmentalism and environmentalists who may answer these questions differently from businesspeople?

As you may imagine, there are many more questions here than answers, and in the next chapter we lay out three alternative views of environmentalism and environmentalists. For the company and the executives who find themselves wanting to move from light green to a darker shade we have two cautions. First, you must be willing to question your basic underlying reasons for such a move because they do not come lightly. Second, engaging the people in your organization in asking how it and they can become more environmentally friendly—to ensure a world for our children—is a process without a clear-cut stopping point. You may begin by trying to turn waste streams into products or by moving into an environmental quality program, and you may well end with a set of philosophical questions about justice and obligations to future generations.

CHAPTER FOUR

Understanding Environmentalism

Introduction

Different shades of green will be appropriate for different organizations. Regardless of the shade, however, managers must make an effort to understand both environmentalists and environmentalism. In chapters 2–3 we have focused on business and how it can be built on environmental values. In this chapter we want to focus on environmentalism and examine some of the underlying values that drive environmentalists.

In chapter 1 we have identified three mind-sets that can serve as a foundation for environmentalism. Each mind-set appeals to basic values, assumptions about the extent of the environmental "crisis," and basic beliefs about the world and the place of humans in it.

The conservation, social justice, and deep ecology mind-sets give rise to a plethora of strategy and tactics used by environmentalists. Executives can only hope to make progress in building cooperative bridges with environmentalists if they try to understand these mind-sets. We are not suggesting that any one of these mind-sets is right or wrong. Nor are we suggesting that particular environmental groups such as Greenpeace, the Environmental Defense Fund, and the like, consciously adopt one of these mind-sets. Rather, we believe that conservation, social justice, and deep ecology represent the range of values and beliefs that form the foundations of environmentalism. We have focused on fundamental values and assumptions about human nature in this chapter. The appendix contains information that is allied with these values and assumptions.

The Conservation Mind-set

The conservation mind-set tells us to conserve the earth's resources for the future. The moral and practical presuppositions for this mind-set are several. First, we have to believe that many of the resources basic to human survival (e.g., clean water, arable land, breathable air, forests, other species) are scarce, a fact the conservationists believe has been amply proved. Second, we have a moral responsibility to future generations and must be willing to frame our activities now in the context of future needs.

The conservation mind-set can be described by outlining the environmental philosophy from which it draws its name. Conservation thinking is particularly identified with a social movement that began at the tail end of the nineteenth century.

America has always been a frontier culture. From the time the first settlers landed on the eastern shore four hundred years ago there has been a continual expansion westward, a progressive conquering of wild places. American culture included a need to push into the wilderness and wrest first survival and then fortune from a recalcitrant nature. Toward the end of the nineteenth century, however, westward progress stopped at the Pacific Ocean, and the frontier as it was then no longer existed.[1]

Yet the frontier mentality remains a part of the American spirit: humans are not dwellers on the land but are temporary fortune seekers who extract the earth's riches and then move on. Increasing control over nature signaled progress: Becoming more civilized meant disconnecting human life from nature more and more, among other things, through the growing industry of creature comforts.

As the last vestiges of the wild west were being transformed into modern culture, a new thinking about the human relationship to the earth began to emerge. The belief in earth's boundless supply of riches began to weaken under obvious signs of irreversible degradation and a dwindling supply of untrammeled land. The recognition of scarcity brought with it the need to parcel out our natural resources. An awakening consciousness of the limitations of our natural resources marked the inception of the conservation movement, which since then has grown and developed as one of our central cultural stories. [2]

Conservation embodied, even in its inception, two competing views about the human relationship to the earth. The first view, often associated with John Muir, was a reaction against the frontier mentality and was concerned with the preservation of nature. The preservationist line developed around the idea that the earth has value of its own, independent of its value to humans, and that the earth's value to humans should be measured in moral, aesthetic, and spiritual terms rather than solely in economic terms. The other view was essentially an outgrowth of frontier thinking. This line of thought, often associated with Gifford Pinchot and called conservation proper, embodied the idea of careful use of our natural resources aimed at development. It focused on economic value and on management policies.

The moral and aesthetic value of nature—the preservationist line—has retained a persistent, though faint, hold on the American mind, particularly as a result of nature writers like Henry David Thoreau, Walt Whitman, Ralph Waldo Emerson, and Aldo Leopold. The preservationist philosophy waned during economic boon times as well as during the two world wars and the Great Depression. It began reemerging in the 1960s, when modern environmentalism became a social force.

The actual lines along which conservation developed, and the program of action for which it lobbied, were actually a far cry from Muir's wilderness vision. The initial impetus behind conservation thinking was the question of forests. What is the value of forests? How should they be used? Should they be saved? Whereas Muir valued forests as wilderness and apart from human needs, most people at the time—including most conservationists—were really interested in how to put the forests to use. What required careful thought was not whether to use the forests but how to use them efficiently and fairly.

Gifford Pinchot (1865–1945), arguably the real father of conservation, had been educated in the European schools of forestry (there were no American forestry schools at the time) and was convinced that the best framework for America's land use policy was the science of forest management.[3] This philosophy of conservation was classically utilitarian, encouraging the wise and efficient use of the natural environment to promote the greatest good for the greatest number of people for the longest time. There was no thought of nature as having value apart from its usefulness to humans. In Pinchot's time there was little compelling scientific evidence that the earth's resources were either limited or nonrenewable. Although waste was discouraged, conservation was not aimed at limiting growth but at continual progress toward the comforts of resource-reliant lifestyles.

The attitudes toward the earth that characterize modern society are rooted in the conservation philosophy adopted under Pinchot's guidance, but there were important elements in the Pinchot-style philosophy that have not filtered down to the present. Because he was civic-minded in his thinking about resource use, Pinchot believed in commercial development. He thought it would lead to benefits for the whole nation, as long as it was placed within a framework of careful national planning and regulation. Pinchot was opposed to the idea of national parks, not because he opposed government control of land but because he feared land preservation that would interfere with commercial use. Attached to the use of natural resources was a strong injunction to be socially responsible, to be acting for the common good. It was the obligation of both government and citizens to manage the nation's wealth wisely, for the good of all and with an eye toward the future.

There is a common perception, particularly among environmentalists, that large corporations are the natural enemies of conservation. Yet this is as untrue today as it was in Pinchot's time. In the early conservation years, business often supported conservation efforts because the movement promised access to the nation's natural riches, particularly mining and timber.

The conservation movement has been closely tied to the interests not only of industry but also of government, which is not to suggest that government and industry always share the same agendas but rather to note tensions within the movement itself. There were ideological differences in how the mandate of conservation—wise use of natural resources—was understood. There was deep ambivalence about government's role, whether and to what degree it should serve as regulator. Sharp differences have always been felt between the ideal of government control aimed at the public interest and the freedom of individuals to pursue their own interests and especially to seek their fortunes in the land. These tensions are still present: a sense of the need for public control is still in tension with a strong attachment to America as the land of opportunity in which each person has a right to seek a fortune on the frontier.

Conservation has always been a mainstream phenomenon. In its beginnings it was not grassroots but represented professional interests. Those involved in the movement have largely been upper middle class, with good access to the processes of economic and political decision making. From its beginnings in the 1890s onward, conservation has had a pragmatic, remedial tone. The philosophy saw no contradiction between environmentalism (as the conservation of resources) and unlimited economic growth.

Conservation was also, in the early stages, a scientific movement. The management of resources was a technical, and not a political issue, best handled by technicians and not legislators.[4] The management of forests was a science, just as the management of personnel is now a science. This attitude has filtered down to us, in a somewhat muddled form. Though environmental issues are often handled by politicians, it is technicians, and the information they compile, that form the basis for what politicians can do. Technical expertise is needed in order to speak with true authority on environmental issues.

Conservation philosophy, even with its internal tensions, is consistent with some of our dominant modes of thought about the environment, and the conceptual resources offered by conservation philosophy are fairly easily integrated. Although there appears to be considerable public debate about "conservation issues" such as spotted owls and logging interests in the Northwest, a broadly shared philosophy lies under the disagreements.

Although some people seem genuinely unconcerned about others, most people have a sense of moral responsibility. And increasing numbers of people seem to feel that the health of our natural environment, as well as the availability of natural resources now and in the future, are moral issues. The conservation challenge is already felt by many of us.

Yet taking conservation quite seriously—particularly in the context of our present ecological situation—will challenge us further. The main conceptual challenge that conservation poses is to expand the scope of moral responsibility. Conservation clearly tells us that we have moral obligations to future generations. The challenge here is to define what the needs of future people might be. We may assume, at the least, that they will need potable water, clean air, an inhabitable climate, land that will produce food, and perhaps even areas of natural beauty. How must we live so that these things will be available to our children and their grandchildren?

As the process of globalization brings people all over the world into relationship with each other, responsibility toward community becomes a more challenging notion. Particularly as we see that the resources to sustain life connect us all—global warming and ozone depletion are the most obvious examples of this—the conservation challenge is one that demands a global view. To preserve a livable atmosphere for our children, we cannot work alone. Likewise, the riches of the earth belong to everyone as a common holding. Thus when we engage in activities that use resources, we must seek to understand impacts, not only on our neighbors downstream but on a global scale as well.

Although such responsibilities are easy to agree with in theory, people who take them seriously find that they add a heavy burden to everyday decision making. If we agree to conserve for the future, for example, it follows that we need a clear knowledge of what resources are available now and what future needs are likely to be. According to conservation, the environment poses countless moral issues, but these concern human relations to other humans. How we treat the earth is not, in itself, a moral issue. We do not have relationships with pine trees or jackrabbits.

Much of the environmental movement and many mainstream environmentalists are conservationists. Since there is no direct contradiction between the conservation mind-set and economic growth, it is easy to see how legal green, market green, and stakeholder green are consistent with the thinking of conservation-minded environmentalists. However, the conservation mind-set does have its limits.

Royal Dutch/Shell, a multinational oil company, recently discovered the limits of its conservation/mitigation-oriented environmental policy in Nigeria. The Nigerian government executed several minority rights activists who had been critical of Shell's activities there. This triggered a review of the company's culture and communications and forced the company to consider its position in Nigeria and other difficult regimes. It abandoned its view that politics, poverty, and minority rights were someone else's problem and equipped itself to deal with them and communicate externally and internally much more effectively in the future. Focusing on conservation can easily raise issues of social justice.

The Social Justice Mind-set

The conservation mind-set is consistent with and maintains our current story about who humans are in relationship to the earth. The social justice mind-set deconstructs this story, suggesting that the story is morally questionable and politically unjust. Whereas the conservation mind-set can be fairly easily identified with a single strand of environmental philosophy, the social justice mind-set is an amalgam of several different philosophies.

Environmentalists with the social justice mind-set draw a direct link between the burgeoning global crisis and a number of mutually reinforcing "ideologies of oppression" (e.g., racism, sexism, speciesism, and classism). In very simplified form, these environmentalists claim that how we act toward the environment reflects how we think about people. It is no surprise that we live in a world marked by both the exploitation of certain groups of people and the exploitation of the earth.

"Environmental racism" is a term that came into use in the 1980s to describe a pattern of practices that placed minorities and the poor at particular environmental disadvantage. Early environmentalists paid scant attention to how local and global inequalities affected and were affected by environmental issues. Environmentalists claim that examples of environmental racism are easy to find and include locating hazardous waste sites in poor communities, lack of attention to green spaces in poor communities, inner city lead poisoning and asthma, siting of industrial activity in poor communities, and nuclear testing near Indian reservations.[5]

Viewed through the lens of the social justice mind-set, many international practices and institutions begin to seem suspect. Global trade patterns—including the push for so-called free trade across borders—signals to some environmentalists the institutional legitimization of economically unjust and environmentally devastating practices. These critics point to the heavy flow of natural resources from South to North, which effectively removes capital from underdeveloped or developing countries while leaving behind greater environmental damages and fewer raw materials. Affluence in the North is paid for elsewhere not only by the outflow of wealth and resources and not only by the exploitation of local cheap labor, but also by the uneven global distribution of environmental deterioration. The world's affluent countries use a vast majority of the world's resources, contributing an uneven share to present and future scarcities; they create the lion's share of pollution, the most toxic of which is often shipped off to poorer nations who will trade their ecological health for money; and they are largely responsible for the most serious global ecological problems, such as greenhouse warming and ozone depletion.

Another facet of the social justice mind-set is ecofeminism. The ecofeminist perspective shows a linkage between the oppression of nature and the oppression of women, arguing that a world which makes sense ecologically will also be a world in which women are no longer exploited or subjugated. Environmentalists who are ecofeminists characterize Western thought as dualistic, so that pairs of ideas are seen in relationship and contrast: spirit/nature, mind/matter, reason/emotion. The first element of the dualism—associated with mind or rationality—has also historically been identified with men. Men, according to this historical narrative, display spirit, mind, reason. Women, on the other hand, have been identified with the second, and lesser, element of the dyad—nature, chaos, fertility, emotion, earth, which has also been considered dangerous and in need of constant control.

Ecofeminists focus beyond these philosophical story tellings, too. They point out various ways in which the exploitation of nature is felt more powerfully, and also more painfully, by women. In many parts of the world the environmental degradation has immediately felt consequences: shortages of food, clean water, and fuel. When food is scarce, women must work harder to provide and will suffer most because they are typically the last to eat. Because women are primarily responsible for child rearing, they tend to have the most vivid experiences of environmental dangers faced by their children. Women are also the target of population control policies. Increased reproductive freedom (including more general access to education, work, and health care) can curb population growth, but many governmental population policies seek greater and greater control over women's bodies and lives.

Ecofeminists point out that modern environmental concern was largely initiated by women and that women have taken a leading role in a majority of grassroots efforts to mitigate or reverse environmental destruction. Although the practical environmental problems of women in industrialized countries may be very different from those of women in developing nations, their agendas are tied in important ways. Any sort of lasting response to the environmental crisis must examine the roots of oppression and must seek changes in the social and political structures that support this oppression.

A final concern of environmentalists operating from the social justice mind-set is the issue of animal rights. Animal rights activists challenge the widespread belief that humans are superior to, and justified in exploiting, other animal species. An unspoken rule in our society is that animals are here for human use and are essentially expendable. Although a certain moral sanction exists against the outright torture of animals, there are otherwise no restrictions on what we can do with or to nonhuman animals: we can eat them, hunt them, do research on them, make them entertain us in circuses, on TV, and in zoos, test products on them, make coats and boots out of their skins, and so on. Yet according to animal rights environmentalists, our society does a grave injustice to animals by using them in these ways.

The environmentalists' argument against speciesism goes something like this: The assumption that only humans matter morally is based on the belief that humans have something which gives them value that nonhuman animals lack—the capacity to reason, to make a free choice, to use language, to have a concept of self.[6] Yet two problems arise for those who deny moral standing to animals. First, it is not clear that animals lack these defining characteristics. Indeed, many scientists who study animal behavior have noted amazing capacities in a number of different species for communication, social relations, and intelligence. Second, if we are going to deny animals consideration because they lack these qualities, we will be forced to also exclude human infants, the senile, and the severely retarded. Once we see that there is no rational basis for denying other animals moral value, it follows that we cannot ethically pursue our own interests by sacrificing the interests of other animals. This is a social justice issue because it tells us that we oppress a certain class of individuals based on prejudice. The just solution to the animal problem would be the immediate abolition of all uses of animals for food, sport, experimentation, or entertainment.

For example, the Body Shop, the United Kingdom-based cosmetics maker and retailer, was forced to change its claim that its products were "not tested on animals" to its being "against animal testing" because it was unable to verify every part of the chemicals supply chain. This high-profile change, however, raised the profile of animal testing issues and forced a number of competitors into better labeling and new sourcing practices. The Body Shop, meanwhile, in spite of various franchising and business difficulties, continues with high-profile social justice campaigns, focusing on animal rights, "trade not aid," rainforest depletion, and other issues.

There are other good examples of businesses profiting from a social justice mind-set. For example, the Co-operative Bank, a U.K. retail bank, sells itself as an "ethical bank" which refuses to lend or invest in companies that have poor environmental records, are involved in oppressive regimes or armaments, manufacture tobacco products, or have inadequate animal welfare. It boasts of rejecting 20 percent of business applications for these reasons. Head of corporate affairs, Simon Williams, states that "we are not doing this as philanthropy or do-goodism or a marketing ploy. There is a deep-rooted belief that there is a business purpose to this—that if we do all these things, better profits will result."

The Deep Ecology Mind-set

For some environmentalists, the social justice mind-set doesn't go far enough. Instead of keeping our present story and instead of trying to change it, even radically, environmentalists with a deep ecology mind-set claim that we need to simply tell a different story of who we are in relation to nature. It seems a simple solution to our problems, yet this different story presents us with the most difficult challenge of all because it calls into question some of our most deeply held assumptions about humans and nature. It also provides us the richest conceptual resources.

Deep ecology environmentalists ground their position in a basic tenet of biology: Homo sapiens are animals and as such are part of nature and depend upon nature for our very existence. Deep ecology environmentalists challenge the belief, present especially in conservation environmentalists, that humans are fundamentally different and distinct from the rest of nature, and somehow exempt from its laws. Human beings belong to nature, and are interdependent with it. Instead of beginning with the question of how best to use nature, this approach begins by asking how best to live as part of nature.

Unlike conservation and social justice environmentalists, deep ecology environmentalists do not have an easily identified history. The moral and spiritual position reflected in this philosophical approach has, according to its adherents, found expression throughout time and across cultures, though it has become increasingly relevant to social problems and social action. As a self-conscious and coherent movement, deep ecology is relatively young. Norwegian philosopher Arne Naess, the first to make an explicit statement of this position, coined the term "deep ecology" in 1972, referring to an environmental ethic that hit at a deeper, more substantive level than others. [7]

Deep ecology is used in a loose way to describe a general attitude or sensibility toward the earth. Many different environmentalists can be called deep ecologists, whether or not they think of themselves in this way. Because deep ecology does not refer to a creed or system of beliefs but rather implies a certain way of thinking about and being in the world, the label has a kind of flexibility.

Most of us go about our lives with a sense of living on the earth rather than being part of it. We may recognize a superficial dependence on nature, albeit one from which technological progress increasingly frees us, but there is nevertheless a philosophical assumption that humans are, at a basic level, exempt from the laws and relationships that characterize the rest of the natural world. According to deep ecology, this belief is part of a larger cultural myth that fuels our environmental crisis. The solution to the crisis will involve both a subverting of the dominant myth about nature and a strong retelling of the stories about who we are and how we fit into the natural world. Since our present modes of thought are incompatible with a sound environmental ethic, we must begin our work at a more basic level by developing a whole new ground out of which such an ethic can flow.

UNDERSTANDING ENVIRONMENTALISM

The "dominant myth" is a philosophical tool for identifying modes of thought that have become embedded in our way of seeing the world. Anthropocentrism, or the belief that the world (indeed the universe) centers around the human species, is central to the myth. Humans are not only superior to the rest of nature, but we are also in essence different from it, for instance, we have consciousness whereas the rest of nature does not. Our distinctness is the locus of valuation: Nature has value only in its usefulness to humans (the most important creatures).

Our cultural myth relies on a set of dualisms: human/nature, spirit/matter, mind/body. According to deep ecology, these dualisms—remnants from the philosophical thought of the Enlightenment—create and enforce a logic of domination because the first half of the dualism is considered superior, and it subverts and controls the lesser half. The human is better than the nonhuman and should control and dominate it.

Other values that we clearly recognize in our thinking are also part of this myth: that technological progress can endlessly improve human life; that the needs and wants of consumer society define who we are; that nature is a "resource." This myth is so deeply embedded that we no longer recognize it as a myth but rather see it as the way things are. Deep ecology seeks to shake the myth loose so that we can examine our unconscious cultural assumptions, particularly those that encourage an exploitative and destructive attitude toward nature.

The retelling of the story within a deep ecology framework looks something like this: All forms of life, both human and nonhuman, have inherent value, meaning that all of nature has value and purpose independent of its usefulness to humans. "Life" is broadly defined to include rocks, rivers, and mountains. And the value of life must be understood not only in terms of individual entities but also in terms of systems, of webs of relationships. A river, for instance, is itself a living thing and is more than just the sum of its parts. The water, fish, rocks, plants, and microorganisms have value and purposes of their own, as does the river as an integrated system.

The central ethical principle of deep ecology is biocentric equality. All parts of the earth's various ecosystems—all life—has equal inherent value and thus an equal right to live and flourish. All entities have a purpose of their own, which is also relevant to the whole of life on this planet. The best way to act is in a way that respects the desire of other life forms to flourish in their own ways. Within a deep ecological framework humans are not omniscient and cannot presume to know what it means for another life form to flourish. Therefore we should practice noninterference whenever possible.

Deep ecology denies the superiority of the human species; all life is of equal value. Nevertheless, the act of living comes continually at the cost of other life forms. Deep ecology resolves this dilemma by asserting that in practice we have a stronger obligation to those nearer us, both in species and in geography. We can affirm that for us human flourishing is top priority without asserting that other beings have less right to blossom in their own ways. Because humans consciously perceive the desire other living beings have for flourishing, we have a responsibility to respect that desire.

The fact that we affirm the right of all things to live and blossom yet must continually thwart other lives in the process of living our own is a conundrum. Instead of being a constant source of guilt, this should provide impetus to distinguish between vital and peripheral needs. Satisfying our vital needs is a positive goal. But sacrificing the lives of others merely for the sake of peripheral needs is wrong. Present human interference with the nonhuman world is unethical precisely because it far exceeds a reasonable fulfillment of our vital needs.

According to deep ecology environmentalists, human flourishing is compatible with the flourishing of the rest of life on this planet, which is quite the opposite of how we often see things. Though deep ecology recognizes that moral dilemmas arise constantly, within this framework it does not make sense to see human life at odds with nature. In fact, truly satisfying ways of human living are those that set human life in a symbiotic relationship with the earth's ecosystem.

Deep ecology places great importance on becoming an ecological self and on developing an "ecological sensibility." Our sense of self begins with the awareness that we are part of nature. Instead of imagining ourselves as simply living "on" the natural world, we recognize a fundamental interweaving of our life with other lives, both human and nonhuman. Self is understood in connection, as something placed, defined by relationships within the ecosystem. Our environment exerts a shaping force on us and is not simply a place upon which we exist.

Deep ecology is essentially about character—a point that marks significant divergence from our first two mind-sets. Our environmental crisis requires a moral shift within individuals, a shift into being people for whom other lives are of profound personal significance.

The meaning of community also changes dramatically. Within a deep ecology perspective, the idea of community broadens to include nonhuman life. There are two layers of meaning in community. First, there is the abstract notion of a global community, encouraging us to think about the impact of our lives in the large picture. Though deep ecology emphasizes the interconnection of humans with the whole earth, it is important to live, day by day, out of a more localized and particularized sense of one's ecological community. This is the second meaning of community: the actual, concrete place where we live. The ethical ideal is "dwelling in mixed communities," which finds practical expression in bioregionalism, where each community's border is defined by bioregion—an area comprising a natural system that is relatively self-enclosed and self-regulating, often delineated by a major watershed or biotic shift, and also by cultural distinctiveness.[8]

Genetic engineering is one area in which we are forced to face up to the deep ecology debate. The genetic engineering of plants is used increasingly to improve yields, quality, shelf life, and other features of plant foods. However, lack of public understanding of genetic engineering, together with mistrust of regulatory frameworks, produces significant resistance to the widespread introduction of genetically modified crops. Monsanto, a leading genetic engineering company, has invested extensively in research and development, testing, education, and public relations. Still, it finds its products and messages mistrusted, particularly in Europe. It is likely that the widespread introduction of genetically engineered food in Europe will take many years and will be accompanied by extensive constraints regarding separation of production and manufacturing, testing, and labeling. Even with those constraints it is very likely that organic or natural alternatives will have to be available.

Genetic engineering goes to the heart of the deep ecology debate. On the face of it, it is a conservationist's dream. It offers the chance of increasing yields and reducing starvation, reducing the use of chemicals in the environment, higher quality, longer-lasting food. Yet, people are inherently mistrustful because it interferes with "the very stuff of life."

Summary

If our argument in this book—that corporations can systematically rethink their strategies in a multiplicity of environmental terms—is successful, then we must follow the logic of this approach. We have argued throughout for an open texture to the greening of business strategy. We must be willing to face the uncertainties wherever they appear.

Environmentalism and environmentalists come in many different flavors. We have identified three of the main mind-sets that underlie modern environmentalism. The lessons for managers are fairly straightforward. If it is assumed that all environmentalists believe the same philosophy, have the same assumptions, or even see the relevant facts the same way, then the conversation between business executives and environmentalists will be brief and pointless.

Executives must understand that many environmentalists see business and economic growth as central to solving the environmental "crisis." Many see business as an anathema, an institution antithetical to even talking about the environment. The basic values and philosophies on which environmentalism is based are conflicting and controversial. Although conservation provokes little disagreement, there is controversy associated with social justice and deep ecology. But no progress will be made if we are close-minded and iconoclastic. We must explore how these and other sets of values would allow us to live.

A student in a classroom in Jakarta, Indonesia, once asked why we were worried about environmentalism at all. According to this student, all three mind-sets reinforced Western dominance and prevented the self-development of other nations. The student pointed out the irony, bad faith, and self-deception of such a view and recommended leaving environmentalism at the border.

Such a challenge should not be taken lightly. What we need is a dialogue, a multifaceted conversation, that can include the three perspectives described here as well as the Indonesian student's challenge. Suggestions for crafting such a conversation are the subject of the next chapter.

CHAPTER FIVE

A Program for Change

Introduction

We have argued that applying the new logic of business, a logic of values, to environmental issues will stimulate a groundswell of creativity. This idea of "creativity through capitalism" is one of the tools we need to meet the challenges posed by our children's future wager. We have suggested four main approaches that companies can take to "green" their business strategy, but as yet we have not addressed the problem of change: how to galvanize support for any particular shade of green. The task of this final chapter is to suggest how people and organizations can put change processes into effect that are self-sustaining.

The New Logic of Business and the Problem of Change

In the old models of capitalism and companies, competitive values and the good of the shareholder almost always won the day. And it comes as no surprise that hundreds of books have been written about the resulting problem of change. If there is little meaning in the work that employees do, little meaning that stems from their own values, then why should they adopt new ways of doing things? If, as Deming suggests, the *actual* main motivation in hierarchical workplaces is fear, we should not be surprised that change is difficult.[1] Change represents new possibilities for failure, and failure and fear are logically connected.

Ironically change programs that use fear, namely, change or

you will fail, may well have more success. We believe that this is the underlying story to Kotter and Hesketh's analysis of why successful culture change is usually accompanied by a crisis.[2] Crises induce fear in general, and fear of failure in particular.

At one level this combination of change and fear is precisely what we see in society's conversation about the environment. If the world is going to hell ecologically, then we had better change before we arrive in that very hot, eternal place. Indeed, this book maintains that it is rational to believe that there is an environmental crisis. But here the similarity ends. Notice that our argument has been not only in terms of any fear you might have for the future but also in terms of something that you care deeply about, your children. It is equally important to note that you care about your children intrinsically, not as means to some other ends. Children are not like meaningless jobs, in regard to which people care about their paycheck and source of livelihood, which they use for other more important purposes.

Where work is built on some values that are intrinsically important to those engaged in the work, change has a different logic. Of course, fear still plays a role, perhaps even terror if we think of threats to our children, but it is a role of catalyzing *action* rather than paralysis. Where values are activated, crises that threaten the values induce action and creativity to preserve them. Change is so embraceable as to sustain itself. Alternatively, where values don't matter, crises induce fear and change is difficult, a problem to be managed and a challenge.

The biggest barrier to implementing a particular shade of green is establishing a set of values that include green values. Imagine a strong values company like J&J or Merck or Levi Strauss deciding to adopt some green values. Of course there would be a lot of conversation about how they were or were not connected to current values, but once that conversation was finished to some satisfaction, the very same spirit of creativity, the innovation mind-set, would take over to begin to realize the green values.

In the new logic of business the problem of change reduces to the problem of establishing values, which is a fairly well understood phenomenon, thanks to our collective experience of rearing our children. In chapter 2 we made some suggestions about how executives could create and sustain enterprise strategy. However, not everyone is ready for a complete commitment to corporate transformation through values, and we want to suggest that there are more modest levers for change. But keep in mind the new logic of business on which they are based. In the following discussion we use the idea of the quality movement as an example, but most of our advice applies to others as well.

Shades of Green and the Quality Movement

Much has been written about the similarity between the environmental problems of business and the quality issue.[3] Many thinkers have proposed a total quality approach to the environment. Incorporating environmentalism into a company's quality process is a good way to start, but only if the quality process is a healthy one.

Training and developing employees with environmental knowledge and technical skills to use the knowledge can unleash their creativity. 3M has countless stories of employees using the quality process to start new businesses that clean up the waste streams of old businesses and make money on their own. It is important to note that values are already operating at 3M.

If you want to use the quality process as an initial leverage point for environmental change, then keep the following questions in mind.

1. Is there a voice mechanism for all employees? Is there a way for people to disagree and to have their disagreements heard and resolved? Without such a process, peer pressure to say the acceptable thing is very great, and creativity and value-added are not often produced.
2. Is there enough technical training? Many executives and employees are woefully ignorant of environmentalism. Does the appendix to this book contain any news for you? It is really the bare minimum of knowledge. If environmental-

ism is to work like quality, then it must be based on "profound knowledge," to quote Deming.[4]

3. Is there a systems point of view? The very idea of a systems viewpoint is present in the concept of ecology. Environmental cause and effect, system logic, and outcomes are notoriously tricky. The science and engineering are often unclear. Training in systems thinking is a necessity if environmental initiatives are to be successful.

4. Are we in it together? If an environmental program is seen as one more thing for employees to attend to but something that executives may forget, then failure will be quick. If environmentalism is important, top management must invest time and attention in it. One executive of an industry that is a major polluter suggested to us that he had nothing to learn about environmentalism, that it would be time wasted in a leadership seminar for the industry. "It's all political now," he said. Needless to say, this company isn't close to the cutting edge in the industry. On the other hand consider the vaunted quality program at Motorola. Robert Galvin, former CEO, talked about quality at every meeting and sometimes left before the financials were discussed.[5]

These questions are general guidelines which, from our experience, serve as necessary ideas if a program of environmentalism, in whatever shade, is to have a reasonable chance of success. Most of these questions stem from a concern with incremental change. Indeed the very idea of quality is built on the concept of continuous improvement. Continuous improvement may be adequate for legal green and market green, but it is probably not enough for stakeholder green and dark green. To begin to realize the values that shades are based on probably requires transformation.

Shades of Green and Leading Transformational Change

Most of our change processes depend on what we have done and where we have been and seek to make small incremental improvements by doing better that which we already know how to do.

Change becomes rooted in the past. The emerging future becomes driven by where we have been.

Transformational change focuses on possibility and vision. It suggests that if we have a clear and compelling idea of the future, of what it is possible to do and where it is possible to go, even though we have never done so before, then that future vision will drive our current behavior. In short, we will create the future instead of allowing it to emerge out of the past.[6]

The first step in leading transformational change is to create *a space of possibility*. Can we engage others in conversations about vision, about a future that we can create? It is here that environmental issues create the first roadblock, for the entire premise of most discussions about environmentalism is rooted deeply in the past, including the language of blame, the politics of guilt and the framework of stopping pollution, cleaning up the mess, and continuing along the same path with minimal environmental damage. How can we even exercise our imagination in such a context? How can we create a future that may well need to be substantially different from the past?

Ironically, some of the most practical ideas about future visions come from very nontraditional business sources: novels and stories. In two books, *Ecotopia* and *Ecotopia Emerging*, author Ernest Callenbach shows us a future that bears little resemblance to our own world.[7] Callenbach suggests that if we see a future in which we live more in tune with the earth, as one of the earth's creatures whose role is not primarily domination and aggression, then we will come to see our relationships with others in qualitatively different ways.

Alternatively, William Gibson, Bruce Sterling, Melissa Scott, and other novelists writing in the genre known as cyberpunk have shown us a high-tech, plugged-in, wired world with environmental devastation, populated by human beings for whom caring, love, and collaboration are exceptions rather than the rule.[8] By focusing on the values that undergird these worlds we can exercise our imagination and see whether we can create a future of our own.

Imagining what is possible for your company cannot single out environmental issues, for a transforming future must integrate these concerns into the very fabric of business and capitalism.

Step two in transformational change is a brutal confrontation with the facts. It is General Electric's Jack Welch, with his idea of candor rather than hope. Welch believes that when we rely on hope we engage in denial about what is really true. Only by being brutally honest can we confront the world as it is rather than as we hope it will be. Where are we? How distant is this vision? And, more importantly, can we commit to the vision?

Many transformational change efforts fail at this point, for step two entails courage. We must celebrate our past and then abandon the past that prevents our vision from being realized. We may envision a world with nonpolluting personal transportation modules, perhaps a sort of "souped-up electric bicycle," yet we may not be willing to give up the conveniences and necessities of the current internal combustion engines on which our society is based. Without paying attention to the facts in a cold and calculating sense, transformational leadership becomes mere dreaming. Practically, this means paying attention to systems. The biggest change lever is aligning systems with vision, for they are notorious artifacts of the past.

The final step in this process is perhaps the most crucial and can indeed overcome barriers in creating a vision for the future and in assessing the present. The final step is best described as pure relentlessness. If A doesn't work to help realize the vision, try B. If B breaks down, then abandon it and try C. It is easy to see that once again the mind-set for innovation must be present.

Transformational leaders and transformational change are rooted in the idea that change is difficult and that people naturally resist change. We want to suggest exactly the opposite. What is difficult is articulating a compelling future. Once such a future is articulated, the change process is self-renewing. Change is difficult only if the future has little meaning other than the present.

When Mohandas Gandhi created a vision of an India united and freed from colonial oppression, the change process became self-renewing and continues today, long after his death. When

Martin Luther King, Jr. created a vision of a society in which African Americans were treated as the equals of white citizens, the need to change wasn't continually resisted by his followers; rather, the process created was self-renewing.

What we need is a conversation about the future that focuses on ensuring that there will be a niche on this planet for our children and their children. If we can have such a conversation, the resulting change process will be self-renewing.

Corporations and executives can lead a microversion of this conversation by engaging themselves in creating a vision of their companies. To the extent that these visions are stakeholder serving, they will contain the seeds for a larger conversation that we most desperately need.

Transformational Ideas for Our Children: Some Speculations about the Future

Our main argument in this book has been that we need to pay attention to a better way to conduct business—a way that takes account of environmental concerns. The logic has been a version of what environmentalists call the Precautionary Principle: Under conditions of high uncertainty and high consequence, we should proceed cautiously to minimize the effects of our action. We have argued further that proceeding cautiously in an environmental sense may well entail proceeding aggressively in a business sense. By urgently pursuing the values on which each shade of green is based, we pursue the results of the precautionary principle by using the innovative and creative engines of capitalism.

Side Bets for Our Children

Another way to put this main argument is to say that we must create our organizations as places in which we want our children to live. By adopting the kind of values-based capitalism that is the fundamental pillar of our approach, companies can ask, What values are necessary to sustain our success? How can we ensure that our children will have the same opportunity for meaningful and exciting work that we have?

Ultimately the test for an ethics of capitalism or an ethics of business must be the test of whether or not we are creating the kind of society we want to pass along to our children. If we are not, then we are erecting even more survival barriers for them.

But what if *Shades of Green* is simply too little, too late? Is there anything else that we can provide in the way of protection for our children's future? Two issues can serve as important "side bets" to place in addition to our children's future wager. Each is relevant to understanding the role of business as an institution that can help protect our place on the earth. And each has the potential to be radically misunderstood in a book about business and the environment.

The Space Colony Side Bet

One real barrier to environmental action is the incredible complexity of ecosystems. Whether we can understand enough about ecosystems in time to repair the damage is not clear. Biodiversity, or rather the disappearance of species, is the prime example. In his famous essay "Is Humanity Suicidal" biologist E. O. Wilson suggests that most of the "maybes" of our children's future wager could be solved if we had the political will and if we allowed ourselves to be creative enough.[9] Contra Wilson and others, we have argued that the institution of capitalism understood as rooted in values must be a vital part of this solution. However, even if we could do what seems impossible, Wilson argues that it may not be enough. Once a species is gone it remains gone. Extinction is forever.

We do not completely understand the role that diversity plays in the rather fragile process of DNA replication called life. How many species are enough to maintain the precarious balance of the ecosystem on earth? We do not know what the answer to such a question would look like, and perhaps we will come to see the balance of life on earth in different terms so that the question of the role of the diversity of life becomes unimportant. Unfortunately, before we reach that point it may well be too late.[10]

If we are rational we must place a side bet, a bet to cover this possibility. We must conduct a natural experiment and create a self-sustaining ecosystem. And we must do it in a sense that cannot easily be undone—as a colony in space. Such a venture could be conceptualized as a way to create value, to understand ourselves better, and to create at least one possible outlet for our children.

The pioneering spirit has been a hallmark of humanity. It is time to reinvigorate it, not in the sense of dominating space as we have dominated the planet but in the real pioneering spirit of people everywhere who have ventured outside their communities to create a better future for their children.

It may seem strange or even fanciful, or, less charitably, naïve and stupid, to talk about space colonies in a book addressed to business executives. But we believe that if such exploration becomes realizable, it will be through the vision of business leaders. Trading off "space exploration" for "meeting the needs of the poor" will never be a feasible governmental policy, nor should it be. The ingenuity and creativity of business is our only possibility. And we must leave this idea here as pure possibility. We are not experts in how to colonize space, but we do know that if we want to ensure a future for our children we must consider all of the possibilities.[11]

The Genome Side Bet

If space colonization is a side bet at the macrosocial level, we need an equally compelling idea at the microlevel—one that helps us to understand, with all due haste, the very processes of life itself. Once again, if we take Professor Wilson's challenge seriously, we will see that it is necessary to understand all that we can about the microprocesses of life.

We must commit to the mapping of the genome, and not just the human genome. We must commit to the further understanding of life processes in their full Darwinian sense. Perhaps we can turn up the light of human reason so that it is bright enough to understand the role of diversity and to better conceptualize the possibilities of our own role in the life process on earth.

If it is possible to understand ourselves as a kind of very complicated "souped-up" chimpanzee, then we need to apply the Socratic dictum "Know thyself." Seeing the biotechnology revolution as one more phase in human self-understanding and extending that revolution to understand the microprocesses of life itself is an important conceptual shift.[12] Such an idea can serve as a value to galvanize further action.

Once again, you may consider it odd to find this idea in a book addressed to business executives. We believe that the current commitment may be too little, too late and that we need to find ways to put more resources into the basic research that is needed. Companies are the only answer that we can see. Can we raise capital to conduct basic research into the nature of life processes and not only with an eye to the development of life-lengthening drugs such as pioneers like Genentech have done?

Again, we are not the ones to define acceptable levels of risk. But as long as we allow research into the basic understanding of life processes to be primarily funded by public resources, we must face the fact that we may know too little, too late.

Some Conclusions

We began this book by asking whether or not it is possible to see capitalism, saving the earth, and creating a better world for our children as forces moving in the same direction. We have provided little in the way of answers; however, our purpose has been to stimulate executives and other business thinkers to engage in a process of asking better questions to help us reconceptualize both our corporations and ourselves.

We want to conclude with some positive steps for action because we believe that we simply must accelerate our attention to environmental concerns. Our suggestions take the form of three sets of recommendations, one each for society, businesses, and individuals. These suggestions are offered in the spirit of creating a space for our children. If you don't like them or even if you think they are stupid and disingenuous, then offer your own.

The Role of Society in a Green Conversation

First, governments need to engage in a process that can separate the damage done to the environment from an analysis of how we have to change to avoid future harms. They must find a way to bracket liability questions and adjudicate them while separating these thorny problems from the regulatory process. And they must seek to invent (not reinvent) and create new modes of governing that enable business and other value-creating organizations to innovate on environmental issues.

Many governments around the world are moving, albeit too slowly, toward such mechanisms. We need not engage in pointless discussion of the purity or impurity of motive around innovations like market-based pollution credits. We need to try them quickly and see if they work and, at the same time, create other mechanisms to accomplish the same results. We cannot afford the wait and bureaucracy that accompanies "the perfect solution." We need to explore the necessity of tax advantages or whatever else it takes for space exploration and for investing in biotechnology.

Second, we need to stop penalizing companies for trying to create value for stakeholders. We need to change the corporate governance mechanisms to more easily accommodate great companies as the model rather than the exception.

Third, governments need to promote the health of their citizens by helping them become environmentally literate. Many governments have successfully used information programs to curb the harmful effects of cigarettes, alcohol, and drug abuse. We need similar attention paid to environmental issues—not only in terms of heartbreaking attention to disasters but real knowledge of our ecosystems and our *biological* heritage. Such a program need not be undertaken in a way that offends the religious sources of many human values. But understanding our biological heritage is necessary if we are to continue to realize these values in ourselves and our children.

Fourth, the third sector—nonprofits, religious organizations, schools, and universities—must join this conversation about the environment. Although this sector has produced many innovative ideas from a panoply of environmental activists, there is more to be done.

Certainly, we can speak for the part of this sector that we know best: the university. Often some of our best minds entrap themselves in medieval structures that pay homage, not to the future and not to our children, but to the historical fact that a group of people happened to have read roughly the same set of books: the disciplines of knowledge. Environmental and ecological issues do not present themselves in disciplinary form. We must find ways to address the issues that have been raised more quickly and much more innovatively.

Finally, our governments and our third sector organizations need to have the same kinds of conversations about green values that we have recommended for businesses. Shades of green apply equally well to these organizations, if we can come to see them as part of the creative solutions that are necessary.

The Role of Business in a Green Conversation

Much of this book has been about how businesses can create a green conversation for themselves, so there is little to add here aside from some very concrete steps.

First, executives need to revisit their mission statement, corporate values, vision, or strategic plan, whichever is appropriate, and ask whether it can serve as a vehicle for creating green, sustainable competitive advantages.

Second, executives must educate themselves and their companies about environmental issues that go beyond the scope of current operations. The extent of this education depends on which shades of green you find compelling, but a little knowledge is dangerous, since you don't know (are not even aware of) what you don't know.

Finally, businesses must drive out the arrogance that comes with the territory of cowboy capitalism. No company and no person is that important in the grand scheme of life. If we are to survive and flourish, it will be from the humility gained by understanding our place in the river of life, not the arrogance and hubris that come from having polluted the river.

The Role of Individuals in a Green Conversation

Ultimately, taking action to ensure a future for our children is up to each of us as individuals. Without individual commitment and concern, societal institutions will always provide too little, too late.

First, we must simply create better governments. The faltering and narrowing civic space described by political theorists must be reopened. Perhaps new information technologies can be a means to that end. However, if we care about our children we will not let apathy or, worse, the hopelessness and despair of others win the day.

Second, we need to think seriously about our responsibilities and the ecological idea that our continuing to flourish is connected to the natural world. Are we aware of the effects of our actions? Are we transmitting this awareness (or lack thereof) to our children?

Third, we need to educate ourselves about ecology and biology. Consumers need to be knowledgeable. So do citizens. It is only by acting our dual role of consumer-citizen that we can influence our companies and our governments to act. By seeing citizenship as the sole province of environmental action we shortchange ourselves and demand too much of our governing institutions.

Finally, we must look into our hearts and try to find a personal vision of the future. What distinguishes us from our chimpanzee and bonobo cousins is our rather sophisticated self-reflexivity— our ability to reflect and question our own consciousness and conscious actions. Without the full power of this self-reflexive ability we simply cannot address the challenge.

Business, human flourishing, capitalism, ethics, and the environment are all ideas that we must put together. We must create new possibilities for understanding ourselves and our organizations. Nothing less than our children's future is at stake.

Appendix

Environmental Challenges to Business

This appendix serves as an overview of our arguments about the environment.[1] It is a kind of primer on the environmental news of the day in which we try to explain some very technical, scientific issues in managerial language. We have tried to cover all of the bases in identifying environmental issues and problems. But remember that there is no one truth about the environment. We will try to give you enough information for you to decide how to place your bets, but there are daily changes.

This appendix deliberately overstates and simplifies the issues. The problems that make up our environmental situation are interrelated and mutually reinforcing; thus, they are hard to separate out into manageable chunks. Separating them for the sake of discussion allows conceptual clarity but risks oversimplification.

Maybe the crisis described in this appendix will never take place. But are you willing to bet your children's future on that scenario? We argue that it is simply irrational to act as if there is no environmental crisis, especially if we can reconceptualize the very institutional engine of capitalism—the modern corporation—to be a constructive force for change.

The "facts" about the environmental situation are not incontrovertible; all of them are politically loaded. Each of the problems we outline involves a controversy over what the facts are and how to read them, and who benefits and who is harmed from a particular interpretation. There is no single correct reading of environmental issues, since the correct reading depends on the purpose for which one seeks understanding. Our descriptions typically reflect the biases of those who are trying to persuade us that there is, in fact, a crisis, though we have also tried to include reasonable instances of skepticism. We have "biased" our presentation intentionally, for we want you, the reader, to decide whether or not this "worst case" scenario is a call to action—a call to rethinking business strategy along the lines we outline in this volume.

It is also important to note that our description of the problems does not imply any particular policy solution. Indeed, our point is that we need to get out of the government/policy gridlock and rethink how we do business. There are no obvious or uncontroversial solutions to any of these difficult problems. The "solutions" involve changing the very modes of thought and being willing to live in a different way. Our solutions involve changing the way that we think and talk and hence changing the very institutions that have given rise to the problems.

The Carrying Capacity Argument: Are There Natural Limits?

Economist Kenneth Boulding asked us to imagine the earth as a spaceship. Every spaceship is a closed system with natural limits as to the number of passengers who will fit on board and the quantity of provisions it can carry. Each spaceship has a "carrying capacity."

One way to describe our current ecological situation is that we have exceeded—or have come very close to exceeding—earth's carrying capacity. Carrying capacity is a term used by ecologists to define the optimal number of a given species that can flourish within a given ecosystem. For example, the carrying capacity for reindeer on a particular island might be around a hundred. When the reindeer population grows beyond this level—say there are now two hundred reindeer—food and habitat sources become scarce and degraded from overuse. The reindeer population then begins to die off, perhaps dropping down to seventy-five before it eventually levels out again at one hundred. The effect of overshooting carrying capacity is a population crash, where a large number of reindeer die off quickly, whether from starvation or exposure.

Perhaps humans, like all other species on earth, are subject to natural limits. Perhaps we too have exceeded earth's carrying capacity. One way to interpret the preponderance of environmental evidence, which we shall shortly present, is that humans are living beyond sustainable ecological limits. This idea of carrying capacity is not just a simple judgment based on the number of people on the planet. [2] Overpopulation may indeed be one of the most profound ecological challenges we face, but it is not numbers alone that strain the earth. Rather, it is a complex interaction of too many people living in ways that tax the earth too heavily—that require too much in the way of resources (food, water, energy, raw materials) and that place too heavy a burden on pollution. The earth cannot replenish or regenerate at our current level of demand.

What is most worrisome is that we seem to be caught up in momentum carrying us toward disaster that may be very difficult to slow. Earth already shows signs of significant ecological distress under the weight of contemporary lifestyles and population. The current population, as estimated by the United Nations, is 5.8 billion, with a third of the population under the age of fifteen. [3] The more conservative estimates of future population growth predict a doubling of the population by the end of the twenty-first century. [4] Because developing countries are expected to contribute about 90 percent of the population growth, those of us who live in industrialized countries tend to think that overpopulation is not our problem. Yet, the population problem is not simply one of numbers but one of lifestyle and values. Both extreme wealth and extreme poverty can be tough on the environment.

Pollution

In one sense all environmental issues come under the heading of pollution, broadly defined. Overpopulation, food scarcity, and the degradation of land are intimately connected with the idea of spoiling the commons. Pollution refers simply to materials in the wrong place and can occur either with the introduction of unnaturally high levels of a naturally occurring substance (quantitative population) or with the introduction of substances that are not naturally occurring (qualitative pollution).[5] The obvious forms of pollution are hazardous substances, solid waste, water, and air.

Hazardous Substances

Hazardous substances are toxic, ignitable, corrosive, or highly reactive materials that pose a significant threat to human health or to the environment. This last clause is important because if a substance is hazardous to the environment there is potential for the environment to harm human health. This connection illustrates the Principle of Connectedness from chapter 2.

Hazardous substances include toxic waste, acids, cyanides, pesticides and herbicides, chlorinated solvents, infectious waste from hospitals and research facilities, formaldehyde, phosgene, fly ash from power plants, and radioactive byproducts from the production of nuclear weapons and nuclear power. Hazardous substances can contaminate ground water and soil, destroy habitats, cause human disease, enter the food chain at all levels, and damage or alter the genetic material of living things.[6]

Hazardous substances include the following:

- *PCBs (polychlorinated biphenyls)* represent a family of over two hundred types of chlorinated hydrocarbon compounds "widely used because of their nonflammable quality as cooling fluid in electrical utility, liquid seals on wood, plastic, rubber and as ingredients in paints, varnishes, inks and pesticides."[7] Both toxic and persistent,[8] PCBs accumulate in fatty tissues of organisms, becoming more and more concentrated as they pass up the food chain. Traces of PCBs have been identified in almost every person tested for them and have been found all over the world in soil, surface water, and fish.[9] They are linked to skin damage, possible gastrointestinal damage, and cancer.[10]

- *Chlorinated solvents* are a major concern as contaminants in drinking water. Chemicals such as trichloroethylene, chloroform, vinyl chloride, carbon tetrachloride, and chlorobenzene are often found in groundwater supplies as a result of leaks, accidents, or simply disposal. Chlorinated solvents induce depression of the central nervous system, cause irritation of tissue, and have been linked to cancer. [11]
- *Pesticides* such as 2,4-D, Captan, Lindane, Disulfoton, and methyl parathion, which are found in both food and water, may cause cancer, birth defects, and liver and kidney damage. [12] Many substances used as pesticides accumulate in the ecosystem over time.
- *Lead* is presently found as a contaminant in drinking water. Lead pipes were outlawed for construction in the United States in 1986, but lead-soldered copper pipes were still used until 1988. Houses painted before 1976 can also be a significant source of exposure because until 1977 lead oxides and other lead compounds were added to house paint. Exposure to lead can damage the central and peripheral nervous system and produces neurotoxic effects like headaches and irritability. Exposure to lead is linked to learning disabilities in children. Other heavy metals such as mercury, cadmium, chromium, and nickel are also connected to lung, kidney, and central nervous system disorders. [13]
- *Radionuclides,* the radioactive forms of certain elements, are produced in mining and milling operations, coal and nuclear power plants, medical facilities, and industrial plants. In 1979, the EPA, citing dangers of cancer-causing radiation, added radionuclides to its list of hazardous pollutants. [14] Dioxins, a family of over one hundred chlorinated hydrocarbon compounds, are notoriously toxic chemical pollutants that bind easily to fat. [15] They are a non-biodegradable byproduct of chemical processes like paper bleaching and waste incineration, and a common ingredient of pesticides and herbicides. Small amounts have caused cancer, immune system depression, and birth defects when

tested on animals, and their effects on humans continue to be studied.

The EPA's position on dioxin is a good case in point of the politically charged nature of "scientific evidence." The EPA announced in June 1988 that its 1985 cancer risk assessment for dioxin 2,3,7,8-TCDD was grossly overstated and that the chemical was only one-sixteenth as potent a carcinogen as previous EPA calculations had suggested. Apparently evidence could not prove adverse health effects of dioxin on humans, even though it was very toxic to other animals. In April 1991, Vernon L. Houk of the Centers for Disease Control admitted that he was wrong in recommending the evacuation of Times Beach, Missouri, in 1982, as well as the $250 million cleanup when the soil was found to be contaminated with dioxin. However, William K. Reilly, EPA administrator, said in August 1991 that reassessment of dioxin was not yet complete and that existing regulations would remain until further research initiatives were completed. Some have argued that in the United States a pervasive fear of cancer has led the EPA to direct its research toward searching for carcinogenic effects and in doing so they have not studied other possible accumulative, long-term effects. When in 1991 the EPA called for a reassessment of dioxin, what it was calling for was a new eye and a new approach to testing the chemical. Environmentalists had been criticizing the EPA for bowing to pressures from dioxin-producing industries when suggesting that dioxin was safer than previously believed. Which side is more credible? Are you willing to bet that one side in this "scientific" controversy is wrong? Wrong all of the time? [16]

The proliferation of hazardous substances in our environment due to human activities is enormous, and the ultimate effects of massive exposure to these substances are essentially unknown and perhaps unknowable. As of 1990, at least 70,000 different chemicals were in regular use, with 500 to 1,000 being added each year. Of these, many have not yet been tested for health and environmental effects. Next to nothing is known about the toxic effects of approximately 38,000 of the more than 48,500 chemicals listed by the EPA. Fewer than 1,000 have been tested for acute effects and 500 for their cancer-causing, reproductive, or mutagenic effects. We believe that this adds evidence to our children's future wager and that it is rational to act as if there is an environmental crisis.

Hazardous Waste

There is a great deal of hazardous material that is left over as the waste from our industrial society. A 1990 estimate for world "production" of hazardous wastes was 360 million metric tons per year. The United States accounts for over 70 percent of the total, more than one ton per person per year. In industrialized countries such as the United States the chemical and petrochemical industries are responsible for an estimated 70 percent of the hazardous waste produced. [17] These numbers don't mean much to us until we have some experience with the difficulties posed by the disposal, storage, and contamination issues raised by the existence of these materials.

The most famous case of the problems with hazardous waste was the Love Canal incident. During the 1940s, the Hooker Chemicals and Plastics Corporation dumped 20,000 metric tons of toxic waste into an old canal, filled in the open site, and sold the land to the local government, disclosing that it did not know what hazards might result. By 1977, it became apparent that toxic chemicals were leaking from the site, contaminating water supplies and homes and causing health problems in the community. Since then, public awareness of chemical pollution has become a top-ranked U.S. environmental concern. [18]

The 1976 Resource Conservation and Recovery Act (RCRA) assigned to the EPA legal responsibility for defining and protecting the public from hazardous wastes. The main task is regulating large companies, which produce 95 percent of these wastes and either treat them or store them on site. Disposal is in secure landfills or by incineration or deep-well injection, and each poses difficulties. Incineration is perhaps the safest but is quite expensive. Injection is only safe in certain geologic formations, and even then is subject to possible blowouts or tremors. Secure landfills face resistance from communities in which sites are or will be located (the NIMBY—not in my backyard—phenomenon) or from towns and cities located along the roads used to transport the waste. It is no wonder that many companies have begun to examine their waste stream to find ways to detoxify it, create new usable products, and otherwise try to rid themselves of both the problems and the liabilities that come with hazardous waste.

A 1989 EPA estimate placed the number of hazardous or potentially hazardous waste sites in the United States at 31,500. [19] By 1989, there were 1,223 priority sites, areas posing imminent and serious danger to human or environmental health, listed by the EPA. [20] The Superfund legislation passed largely in response to Love Canal and reauthorized in 1986 is the government's main tool for identifying and cleaning up these toxic dumps. However, the money earmarked by Superfund is simply not enough to clean up all of these sites. The original budget of $4.1 billion was cut to $1.6 billion in order to pass as a law. Although the original sponsors of the law had hoped to avoid litigation battles, which can often tie a law into inaction, those battles broke out. As of 1991, only thirty-three sites recognized as priority projects ad been deemed fully recovered, with over 1,200 others on the list. [21]

The storage and disposal of toxic material has generated its own industry. Many cities and states transport their wastes across state lines to places where land is cheap or "undesirable." And there seems to be a growing trade in illegal international shipments, particularly to so-called third world countries. The case of the freighter *Khian Sea* epitomizes the plight of toxic waste for which no one wants responsibility. The ship set sail from Philadelphia in August 1986 and roamed the seas for two years looking for a place to unload its cargo of 14,000 tons of toxic incinerator ash. Finally in February 1988, under the pretense of delivering fertilizer, the *Khian Sea* dumped 3,000 pounds of its toxic cargo in the rural Haitian port of Gonaives. The remaining cargo found its way, illegally, into the ocean. [22]

Disposing of nuclear waste is especially troublesome because of the persistence of radioactivity. Even low-level waste remains radioactive for sixty to three hundred years, and high-level wastes like spent fuel rods from reactors remain radioactive for thousands of years. The U.S. government has unsuccessfully tried for years to find a permanent solution to this problem, but it turns out, once again, that the government is part of the problem, not the solution.

A GAO investigation into the Department of Energy's nuclear weapons facility at Hanford, Washington, showed that the radiation level of the drinking water in the surrounding community was four hundred times greater than the proposed drinking water standard at the time. As it turned out, thousands of curies of radioactive iodine had been secretly released. [23] The Rocky Flats plant near Denver, Colorado, the country's only source of plutonium for weapons (for warheads as in the Trident 2 missile), has had sustained problems with leakage. [24]

The potential for devastating accidental releases of toxic substances exists. Probably the world's worst chemical accident occurred at Bhopal, India, in 1984. More than 3,000 people were killed and 20,000 suffered serious injury when a deadly cloud of methyl-isocyanate leaked from a Union Carbide pesticide plant. [25] In July 1991 along the Sacramento River in northern California 19,000 gallons of metam sodium, a powerful pesticide, spilled into the river when the train transporting it went off the tracks. In concentrated form, metam socium can be fatal if splashed on the skin, and can damage eyes and lungs. Hundreds of thousands of fish were wiped out in a forty-five-mile stretch of river, and almost all plant life was killed. [26] Several nuclear disasters or near disasters have also become lodged in the public consciousness, particularly the catastrophic disaster at Chernobyl in 1986, which released 185 million curies of radiation and caused an estimated 600 to 32,000 deaths according to the Ukrainian ambassador to the United States. The large magnitude of difference here is more evidence of the uncertainty that we face, as increasing rates of thyroid cancer in children and immune difficulties in those involved in the cleanup of Chernobyl are only gradually becoming apparent. [27]

Oil spills are also cases of chemical accidents. The Exxon *Valdez* spill, to which we referred in chapter 1, spilled 11 million gallons of crude oil into Alaska's Prince William Sound in March 1989. By January 1997 the ecosystem had still not recovered and, according to one report, only one species, the bald eagle, had fully recovered from the impact. [28] In February 1983, an offshore well in the Nowruz oil field in the Persian Gulf collapsed, spilling twenty times more crude oil into the water than did the Valdez. And, in June 1979, an oil well at Intoc 1 on the Yucatan Peninsula exploded, spilling 200 million gallons. Reports of smaller spills make the back pages of the newspapers with alarming frequency, and many more go unreported.

Oil and other chemical spills in the ocean represent one of the largest contributions to water pollution. In 1988, there were 5,000 to 6,000 spills involving oil or other toxic substances. Twelve of these involved more than 100,000 gallons. According to data from the Coast Guard's pollution incident reporting system, 91 million gallons of oil and 36 million gallons of other toxic substances had been spilled into U.S. waters between 1980 and 1986. [29] Between 1973 and 1989, large tanker ships spilled some 870 million gallons of oil and other petrochemicals. [30] One estimate is that in 1996 over 6 million tons of oil entered the world's oceans, partially coming from spills as well as from coastal refineries and ships' bilges. [31]

War and ecoterrorism pose different but related issues, since environmental damage from war is hardly accidental. Though often labeled as "incidental," it is real nonetheless. Two pesticides used in the Gulf War, DEET and permethrin, have been found to be harmless when used independently, but in combination may cause many of the symptoms that have been termed Gulf War syndrome, including memory loss, headache, fatigue, muscle pain, and tremors. [32] In the wake of the Persian Gulf war some two hundred lakes of oil formed in the desert, some of them more than a mile wide and several feet deep. Altogether they contained 30–60 million barrels of oil. [33] Oil evaporates to leave a thick poisonous residue of fuel oil and gas oil that seeps into the ground. In addition to the oil lakes, there were at least 450 oil well fires. Smoke in such quantity may obscure the sun sufficiently to cause changes in climate patterns, and it releases emissions of sulfur dioxide—which causes acid rain—and carbon dioxide, which may contribute to global warming.

Pesticides

Since pesticides are found in what people feed themselves and their children, they are one of the toxic substances that worry people the most. As is typical of the issues we have outlined in this chapter, the pesticide question produces radically opposed perspectives. Some see their use as causing an insidious poisoning of the population by profit-seeking agribusiness and a complicit government. For others, pesticides hold the key to providing sufficient food to the people of the world.

Pesticides have been used throughout recorded history. The first Federal Insecticide Act was passed in 1910. Public awareness of it as a potential environmental hazard mushroomed after the publication of Rachel Carson's *The Silent Spring* in 1962, describing how pesticides, particularly DDT, were accumulating in the food chain and causing ecological damage.[34]

Pesticide use in the United States has grown from a yearly application of 300 million pounds in 1966 to well over a billion pounds today.[35] The EPA now lists some 25,000 pesticides in use in the United States while a different source places the number of different chemical formulations on the market at 37,000.[36] The accumulative effects of such massive deployment of chemical weapons against insects, plants, and animals is far from clear.

Environmental and consumer advocacy groups claim that the EPA and the FDA, the two federal agencies authorized to monitor and control pesticide levels in our food supply, are not doing their job. Many chemicals used on crops have not been tested for safety. Only 10 percent of the seven hundred biologically active ingredients monitored by the EPA, and none of the 1,200 inert ingredients, have been adequately tested for toxic effects.[37] As of May 1990 at least twenty-seven pesticides approved for use in the United States were listed by the EPA as probable human carcinogens. [38] The FDA tests less than 1 percent of domestically grown produce for pesticide contamination and less than 1 percent of the produce imported from other countries. Recently the EPA has announced that the study of hormone disruptors will be made a top priority in the testing of chemicals, which raises questions about the depth and expanse of testing in the past. [39]

The EPA does occasionally recommend strict regulation, for example, a ban on ethyl parathion, one of the family of insecticides called organophosphates. The EPA estimated that ethyl parathion had poisoned more than 650 field workers in the United States (more than 100 fatally) since 1966. It is used on about fifty different crops, including apricots, broccoli, lettuce, onions, and wheat. [40]

In California methyl bromide helps to produce 80 percent of the U.S. supply of strawberries grown there. Methyl bromide in substantial amounts is highly toxic but is used throught the country on tomatoes, tobacco, and grapes. Bromide is also very efficient in ozone, even more so than chlorine, though it is broken down more readily than chlorine. According the U.N. Montreal Protocol, methyl bromide is to be phased out by 2010, though there is much controversy around the economic feasibility of such a ban. [41]

Even when chemicals are banned in the United States, manufacturers can export to developing nations that control pesticides less rigorously. DDT and BHC, though illegal in the United States and much of Europe, still account for three-fourths of all pesticide use in India, despite their known carcinogenic effects. Aldrin, dieldrin, heptachlor, chlordane, and kepone have all been banned in the United States but are used in Equador, Guatemala, and Costa Rica on cocoa, coffee, and bananas that are imported to the United States. In a March 1990 report, the GAO identified 110 pesticides that the EPA has not approved for use in the United States but are registered in exporting countries. It is far from clear that our food supply is as safe as we are led to believe. [42]

One estimate places the number of pesticide poisonings each year between 400,000 and 2,000,000, one-fifteenth of which result in death. [43] Most of these exposures occur in developing countries where farmers and workers do not take safety precautions because they are uninformed and unequipped. There are other problems with pesticides that should give us pause for thought:

- Pesticides are often broad-spectrum products that kill not only the target pests but their natural enemies as well, which can create a cycle of dependency on pesticide use.
- Some of the chemicals used go through processes of biological amplification, accumulating in animal and human tissues.
- Groundwater contamination is a problem because residues from pesticides remain in topsoil and are carried through by excess water into the groundwater. The EPA has found seventy-four different pesticides in the wells of thirty-eight states.
- Long-term human health effects from pesticide residues in our food and water yet present unknown dangers.

The supporters of pesticides claim that they save millions of lives by killing disease-carrying insects, increasing the food supply, lowering food costs, and generating increased economic benefits for society. They are constantly trying to develop safer products to replace potentially dangerous ones. The industry has responded to the threat of accidents and misuse with a comprehensive program known as Responsible Care.

Endorsed by over forty partners of the Chemical Manufacturers Association, Responsible Care attempts to open the chemical manufacturing business to the public and other stakeholders in the companies. The program focuses on health and safety. It calls for working toward the reduction of waste and emissions, the safety of workers, the safety of products in all phases of manufacturing and distribution and use, and for solving the problems of past products and the issues of waste disposal. [44] Whether this program is enough either in terms of rebuilding the image of the industry or in putting enough controls in place is an open question.

Solid Waste

Solid waste is any unwanted or discarded material that is not a liquid or a gas. The United States creates over 450,000 tons of residential and commercial solid waste each day. A large portion is produced by processes such as mining and producing oil and natural gas, and is stored or discarded on site, creating potential problems with air, water, and soil pollution.

About 80 percent of U.S. municipal trash is simply dumped into landfills. [45] There is a continuing need for new sites, but strong resistance from community members makes new locations difficult to find. The Resource Conservation and Recovery Act of 1976 banned open dumping and required sanitary landfills, in which wastes are spread in thin layers, compacted, and covered with dirt daily. Although sanitary landfills are much less offensive to neighboring communities, contamination of surface water and groundwater is again a serious hazard—the EPA has already identified over one hundred potentially harmful substances in landfill leachate. The EPA also estimates that U.S. landfills emit about 200,000 metric tons of volatile organic chemicals that affect atmospheric ozone and ground-level smog concentrations and pose a fire hazard. [46] Recent research done at the University of Maryland on two landfill sites in Maryland outside the Washington Beltway revealed that both were emitting approximately three hundred tons of smog-forming gases such as ozone and seventy-five tons of hazardous air pollutants each year. These emissions are well above the amount regulated by the Clean Air Act of 1990.[47]

Water Pollution

Many have argued that most, if not all, of our water is contaminated, and new sources of pure water, especially fresh water for drinking, are seriously limited. Of all the water on earth, 97.5 percent is salt water and 2.5 percent is fresh. [48] Oceans, lakes, streams, deltas, estuaries, and aquifers all show the negative effects of human activity. That many Americans are aware of this is evidenced in the explosive growth of the bottled water industry, as more and more people distrust their usual source of the well-spring of life.

Major water pollutants include disease-causing agents (mainly from human and animal waste), organic chemicals, sediment, radioactive substances, and inorganic plant nutrients such as fertilizers. There are countless sources of water pollution, many of which we have identified in earlier sections.

For purposes of monitoring and regulation, water pollution in the United States is divided into point and nonpoint sources. Point sources, such as factories and sewage treatment plants, discharge pollutants at specific locations (for instance, a pipe emptying into a river or an ocean). These are fairly easy to monitor. Nonpoint sources are large land areas such as farms, feedlots, parking lots, and construction sites, where runoff creates a broad and diffuse source of contamination that is difficult to monitor and control. Agriculture is the primary source of nonpoint pollution. It includes rainfall runoff from areas of high waste concentration like barnyards and feedlots, and rainfall and irrigation water washing across farmland and picking up chemicals, especially nitrogen and phosphate fertilizers, and pesticides. Other sources are forestry operations, construction, mining, and urban runoff. [49]

Rivers are contaminated by both point and nonpoint sources of pollution. Often sewer lines and drainage pipes from industries pour huge quantities of untreated waste into rivers. Large and fast-flowing rivers have a fairly good ability to recover from most kinds of pollution, though even the largest rivers are sometimes so overloaded that they begin to suffer. Lakes are usually more seriously affected, both by outright dumping and by air pollution. Eutrophication, which is caused by nitrate fertilizers and phosphates, is a common problem in lakes and can destroy the entire ecosystem of a lake. In the United States it is estimated to be a problem in 48 percent of lakes and reservoirs. [50]

Coastal and inland wetlands, which play an important role in replenishing groundwater supplies, filtering pollutants from lakes and rivers, and buffering the effects of storms and floods, are rapidly being destroyed (recall the principle of connectedness). The United States has already lost half of its wetlands to drainage, construction, or pollution, and current annual loss is estimated at 450,000 acres. [51]

Oceans are perhaps our most polluted waters, since they serve as a global dumping ground for everything from the daily garbage of boats to millions of tons of dredge spoils. The oceans are polluted by agricultural and industrial runoff discharged by rivers and streams, by sulfuric and nitric acids from acid rain, by toxic chemicals from wind-borne pesticides, by oil spills from tankers and drilling rigs, by tons of garbage, mainly plastics, dumped by ships, fishermen, and recreational boaters, by raw human and animal sewage, by radioactive wastes, by toxic ash (dioxin) from ocean incinerators and illegal dump ships, and by medical and surgical debris.

Groundwater—the freshwater stored in aquifers beneath the earth's surface—is perhaps our most precious but least protected resource. Pollution comes in the form of microbiological contaminants, toxic and inorganic chemicals, and seepage of pesticides and herbicides. There are at least 10,000 underground gasoline tanks with the potential to leak petroleum products into groundwater. Saltwater is migrating into overpumped aquifers along the coast and because aquifers do not flow like rivers, contamination is thought to be essentially permanent. [52] And aquifers can be depleted. The Ogallala aquifer, which underlies 170,000 miles of the Great Plains and is the largest U.S. groundwater source, is being depleted much more quickly than it can be replenished.

Air Pollution

Pollen dispersal, wind erosion of soil, and fires caused by lightning are all natural sources of air pollution. At low levels, the atmosphere is able to cleanse itself, but human activity has dramatically increased the quantities of some naturally occurring air pollutants and has added massive new sources. Air pollution has serious short- and long-term health effects on humans and other life forms, and it is intimately linked to many other facets of our environmental problems: global climate change, stratospheric ozone depletion, water pollution, acid rain, loss of forests, and damage to crops.

Almost every large human population center on the earth has a problem with air pollution. In places such as Los Angeles, New York, and Denver, air pollution noticeably lowers the quality of life, through ill health and forced changes in lifestyle, such as having to avoid outdoor physical activity. In the United States alone, over 150 million people breathe air that is considered unhealthy by the EPA.

The most common and widespread pollutants emitted by human activities in the United States are sulfur oxides, nitrogen oxides, carbon monoxide, ozone, suspended particulate matter, lead, and volatile organic compounds. The Clean Air Acts of 1970 and 1977 require the EPA to establish and monitor national ambient air quality standards for these seven major outdoor pollutants. The vast majority of air pollution comes from burning fossil fuels in power and industrial plants and in internal combustion engines in motor vehicles. Organic vapors from paint, dry cleaning chemicals, and charcoal starter fluid on the backyard barbecue also contribute to air pollution.

Photochemical smog—the yellow haze that sits over Los Angeles—is a particularly harmful component of air pollution, formed by the reaction of strong sunlight on a mixture of nitrogen oxides and volatile organic compounds. The main sources of smog are unburned hydrocarbons in fuel tanks and industrial processes. [53] Ground-level ozone is the most harmful and widespread component of smog. Ozone is toxic on contact to most living organisms. It causes eye irritation and respiratory problems in humans, and it damages leaves and slows the growth of plants, reducing crop yields.

Nitrogen dioxide is also associated with damage to the lungs and bronchial passages. Suspended particulate matter—pieces of ash, soot, dust, or liquid droplets released into the air—pose a danger because they can be ingested or can lodge in the lungs.

Other pollutants pose similar health risks, particularly to respiratory functions. Not only is there a correlation between air pollution and respiratory ailments, but research is now showing possible connections to heart disease, cancer, and a weakened immune system. [54]

But ecosystems can be damaged at lower levels of pollution than those harmful to humans. Long-term exposure to air pollutants interferes with photosynthesis and plant growth and causes direct damage to leaves and needles. Acid deposition caused by air pollution damages forests and has a profound impact on the aquatic life of freshwater lakes and streams. Many species of wildlife suffer both immediate effects of air pollution and the indirect effects of lost and damaged habitat.

Since the passage of the Clean Air Act in 1970, the EPA has made progress in reducing levels of many pollutants. Concentrations of lead, for instance, have dropped dramatically. Concentrations of ozone and suspended particulate matter, on the other hand, have increased. A 1990 *New York Times* article reported scientific studies showing the presence of more than three hundred potentially dangerous airborne pollutants being breathed by Americans. Of these three hundred only seven are regulated by government. [55]

A Reprise of Our Children's Future

We are not suggesting that the harms outweigh the benefits of the chemicals and processes that produce pollution, nor that the benefits outweigh the harms. We are suggesting that enough questions have been raised for us to consider that it is rational to bet that there is an environmental crisis. Furthermore, it seems to us that far from being the solution to the crisis, government is often part of the problem.

If this logic is correct, then we must find a way to reconceptualize business to make environmental values a central part of capitalism instead of an add-on to be used to justify cleanup costs, regulations, and other ineffective institutions.

APPENDIX

Human-Induced Global Climate Change Scenarios

Global warming and the greenhouse effect are highly charged labels for one of our most controversial environmental issues, for some, the most critical and life-threatening crisis ever to face the human race. To others, it is unsubstantiated alarmist hype. The issue is difficult to assess because so much scientific uncertainty and disagreement surrounds the question of whether there is a problem and if so what it is. The difficulties are compounded when people are suspected of choosing the scientific evidence that supports their favorite policy. Indeed this issue illustrates the morass surrounding environmental policy that we mentioned earlier. In keeping with the spirit of this chapter, we are going to present the "facts" as they are described by those who consider human-induced global climate change to be at least a potential environmental threat.

The moderate temperature that allows life on earth to flourish is made possible by a natural process, sometimes labeled the greenhouse effect, whereby trace atmospheric gases trap heat near the earth's surface. As concentrations of carbon dioxide, water vapor, and other "greenhouse" gases in the atmosphere increase, there may be a corresponding increase in the amount of heat trapped, and hence an overall warming of the earth's surface temperature. At issue in the global warming question is not whether there is a natural greenhouse effect but to what extent human activities are altering the earth's natural balance and what the consequences of these alterations will be.

Next to water vapor, carbon dioxide is the most plentiful greenhouse gas (though it amounts to a mere 0.035 percent of atmospheric gases). It has long been considered the central problem in global warming scenarios. The concentration of carbon dioxide in the atmosphere is, in fact, steadily increasing. Atmospheric concentration is believed to be 25 percent higher now than it was before the Industrial Revolution, and if current trends continue, concentrations will jump 75 percent by 2060. [56] Carbon dioxide occurs naturally but is produced in large quantities by human activities, especially through the combustion of fossil fuels.

Deforestation is believed to account for 20 percent of the increase in carbon dioxide. [57] Because plants absorb carbon dioxide and convert it into oxygen through photosynthesis, reducing the number of trees increases carbon dioxide levels. It is released when forests are burned and when they are cut, since carbon dioxide is then released from the soil.

Some scientists are suggesting that other gases—specifically methane, nitrous oxide, and tropospheric ozone—actually trap heat more effectively than carbon dioxide, and may well present more serious environmental threats. Methane concentrations have increased by 100 percent in the last 150 years. [58] Levels of tropospheric ozone are also growing, primarily due to the burning of fossil fuels. In addition a class of synthetic chemicals called chlorofluorocarbons (CFCs), which are not normally found in the atmosphere, are thought to affect greenhouse gases. Concentrations of CFC-11 and CFC-12, the two principle fluorocarbons affecting greenhouse gases, are increasing at a rate of 5 percent annually. [59]

At the end of the century, there is widespread agreement among scientists that global warming is a real phenomenon and could have dramatic consequences. Few doubt that humans' putting carbon dioxide into the atmosphere at the record rate of 6.3 billion tons per year is not sustainable. According to some reports, there is a consensus in the scientific establishment that we are already committed to a temperature increase of 0.5–1.5 degrees centigrade based on the buildup of gases since 1860 and that we will likely see a global average temperature increase of 1.5 to 4.5 degrees centigrade over the next century if current emission trends continue. [60]

Even though there is more agreement than ever about global warming, the timing and the magnitude of the warming are highly uncertain. The 1980s and the 1990s were the warmest decades on record, but scientists admit that there is no "proven connection" between the warm weather and a pattern of global warming. Some scientists go so far as to say definitively that there is no global warming. [61] To them, the unusually high temperatures merely give alarmists opportunity to press for changes that might not ultimately be in our best interests and will, in the short run, be bad for the economy.

Making the issue even more controversial is the fact that predictions of global warming are based on computer-simulated global models, the accuracy of which are questioned by people both within the scientific community and at large. Even among those who agree that temperature changes are occurring, or will occur, there is little agreement on what the effects of these changes will be. There will most likely be alterations in moisture patterns, affecting both agricultural productivity and sea levels. Some potentially negative effects predicted by scientists are melting of the polar ice caps, erosion, or inundation of agriculturally rich coastal areas and salinization of coastal freshwater lakes and aquifers. It is possible to argue that changes in the earth's surface temperature are not necessarily bad, since warmer weather may mean that we could produce more food. It is also possible that some places will be cooler, some dryer, some wetter, and the cloud cover could increase to offset warming.

Global warming illustrates the central question of this book: How are we, who are not technical specialists, to act when faced with contradictory scientific evidence and when concerned about the legacy we leave for our children? The stakes are high, and inaction represents one all-too-easy response.

Stratospheric Ozone Depletion

There is a crucial difference between what we might call good ozone—stratospheric ozone that provides a life-sustaining protective layer from the sun's radiation—and bad ozone—ground-level ozone, the main component in urban smog. Concerns over ozone depletion and ozone holes refer to good ozone and to speculations that human activities are destroying something vital to our continued existence. However, like the controversy between good and bad cholesterol, there is usually a great deal of confusion.

A natural layer of ozone lies between nine and thirty miles above the surface of the earth, creating a shield against the sun's harmful ultraviolet rays. The three-atomed oxygen molecule is the only gas that absorbs much of the hazardous ultraviolet radiation that destroys life, leading scientists to speculate that decreases in ozone concentrations could have adverse effects.

Several compounds directly related to human activities have been found to affect the ozone layer in a number of ways. CFCs are considered the most harmful, since they break down and release chlorine atoms when they encounter high-energy ultraviolet radiation in the stratosphere. Each chlorine fragment released can destroy up to 100,000 ozone molecules. [62] Scientists estimate that 80 percent of the destruction of the ozone layer is caused by CFCs and other chemicals such as methyl choloroform and carbon tetrachloride. [63] Halons—found, like CFCs, in air conditioners aerosols, rigid and flexible foams, refrigerators and freezers, cleaning solvents, and fire extinguishers—are also implicated in ozone depletion.

In 1985, British scientists discovered a huge hole in the ozone layer over Antarctica. The hole, which has been observed each spring since 1985, may represent a 50–60 percent depletion of ozone. [64] This was the beginning of recent public concern over ozone depletion, leading to the Montreal Protocol, a 1987 agreement originally signed by twenty-four countries to halt the production of CFCs by the year 2000. By 1996 over 140 countries had adopted the protocol. Concern over ozone depletion has increased in some circles, since the world's output of ozone-depleting chemicals is still high. Concern has decreased in others, since the Montreal Protocol has actually succeeded in reducing emissions, and most countries seem willing to continue in this direction.

Depletion of the ozone layer poses several known health and environmental threats. Increased radiation leads to a higher incidence of skin cancer and possible eye damage; human and animal immune systems are disrupted; growth processes of plants are interfered with. One recent report cited reduced algae growth in the ocean as the first evidence that the ozone hole is affecting life.

Scientists recorded a 2–4 percent reduction in total annual growth of oceanic plankton, an organism that forms the base of the Antarctic food chain. [65] Once again we are left with controversy as the only reasonable conclusion to draw, and once again we are left wondering about our children's future as a wager about the environment.

Degradation of the Land

Environmentalist and farmer Wendell Berry once said that life depends on six inches of topsoil and the fact that it rains now and then. However, we tend to view land as both a renewable and an unlimited resource, but neither is actually the case. In the following discussion we examine three threats to the land: loss of Topsoil, deforestation, and desertification.

Loss of Topsoil

Each year millions of tons of soil, disrupted by erosion or qualitative deterioration, are washed or blown away. Although talking about a shortage of dirt may seem strange, it is becoming clear that soil is one of our most valuable and most threatened resources. We know of no way to replace soil once it is lost. The most obvious effect of this degradation is the threat to our ability to produce food: globally about 11 million hectares of our arable lands are lost each year. If the current trend continues, by 2000 we will have lost about 18 percent of our arable lands. [66]

Soil erosion is a natural process that occurs when wind or flowing water washes away exposed soil. Under normal conditions, topsoil regenerates at about the rate it is lost. Human activities have so greatly accelerated erosion that topsoil is eroding faster than it can be replaced on about 35 percent of the world's cropland. [67] Overgrazing is the main culprit in the degradation of land, since loss of vegetation exposes soil to water and wind erosion. Overfertilization (leading to soil acidification), inexpert irrigation, inadequate terracing of steep slopes, and leaving cropland exposed during fallow periods lead to damaged land and reduced crop yields. Deforestation causes both erosion and water contamination. Logging, construction, and mining operations can cause severe erosion. A 1992 report by the United Nations estimated that 10.5 percent of the earth's most productive soil has been severely damaged by human activity since World War II. [68] The study points to as much as 22 million acres of land that is now unreclaimable, in addition to another 3 billion acres of land that can be reclaimed only at great cost. The United States loses over 1 billion tons of topsoil per year and one-third of our cropland is now in marked decline due to soil erosion. [69]

Deforestation

Forests play an invaluable role in the functioning of the earth's ecosystem. Tropical forests, particularly, are a major source of biological diversity. Forested watersheds recharge and cleanse streams, springs, and aquifers. Because forests are crucial in maintaining global and regional climate, they are crucial to world food production. Trees also prevent soil erosion, and they absorb noise and air pollution. Human uses for forests include fuel, lumber, paper, and medicines. It is estimated that one quarter of all prescription and nonprescription drugs, and 70 percent of the promising anticancer drugs being researched, are derived from plants in tropical forests. [70]

Forests are being destroyed worldwide. Each year, an area of forest at least the size of England is eliminated. Most of the destruction is occurring in the moist forests and open woodlands of the tropics. In 1950, 30 percent of the earth's land was covered by forests; by 1975 it had dropped to 12 percent; by 2000 it will likely be only 7 percent. By some estimates our tropical forests may disappear entirely by 2050, with the possible exception of sections of western Amazonia and the Zaire basin. [71]

The most serious threat to the forests is the growing demand for agricultural land. Traditional "slash-and-burn" agriculture, which can be a sustainable use of the forest at low population densities, is highly destructive when carried out on a large scale. These agricultural practices account for the destruction of 5 million hectares per year, as well as the degradation of an additional 10 million hectares. [72]

Madagascar, one of the most striking examples of deforestation, is a biologically rich and diverse area. About 85 percent of the original forest cover is gone. In the Peten area of Guatemala, home to most of the second-largest rain forests in the southern hemisphere, 60,000 hectares of jungle disappear each year. The forests of Palawan in the Philippines have lost half of their original cover. The Lacandona jungle in southern Mexico, the largest remaining tropical forest in North America, has been cut to half its original size.

Desertification

Desertification refers to the deterioration of ecosystems and the destruction of their biological productivity. The 1977 U.N. conference on desertification defined it as "the diminution or destruction of the biological potential of the land, which leads ultimately to desert-like conditions" and spoke of it as "an aspect of the widespread deterioration of ecosystems under the combined pressure of adverse and fluctuating climate and excessive exploitation." [73]

The concept of desertification presents certain difficulties. Some ecologists and biologists consider the term itself misleading. It does an injustice to deserts which, not at all lifeless, can be enormously complex ecosystems. Much of the talk about desertification frames the problem as "the encroaching deserts," suggesting that deserts themselves are expanding, which is highly controversial. The shape of deserts tends to change over time, under wholly natural conditions, but evidence to show that the world's deserts are actually encroaching on nondesert areas is not terribly convincing. Controversy over the term aside, there is widespread agreement that huge areas of land are becoming less arable due to human activities. This is the heart of the concern over "desertification."

Of the earth's ice-free land area, those concerned say that one-third is affected or likely to be affected by desertification. [74] Each year 12 million hectares deteriorate to the point of being agriculturally useless. Devegetation can be caused by climatic variations but is more often the result of overgrazing or exposure of topsoil through cultivation. Deforestation without regeneration is an additional factor. The potential threat to human well-being is immense: 230 million people are directly threatened by desertification, specifically by the decreased potential for food production.[75]

The predicted global consequences of desertification include increases in atmospheric dust, changes in hydrological systems, climate change, loss of genetic diversity, and a reduction of the productive base of society. Because of these environmental effects desertification is likely to cause social and political instability.

Biodiversity

Both diversity of species and genetic variability among individuals within a particular species are crucial to the survival of life on the planet. Both are in danger from human activities, and many biologists consider this to be the fundamental environmental crisis facing us today.

The rapid loss of species threatens small-scale and large-scale ecosystem stability. We need diversity of species, first, because of the interdependencies that link flora and fauna. Beyond this, reduction in numbers within a species can lead to the loss of races and varieties, leading to a loss of genetic diversity. The loss of genetic diversity is at least as threatening as the loss of species because variation within species allows them to adapt to environmental challenges. A species that is dramatically reduced in numbers and loses genetic subunits (races, populations, etc.) becomes vulnerable to habitat destruction, climate change, and disease.

The tragedy of extinction cannot even be fully felt, since we have little idea of what we are destroying. We can be sure, though, that we are denying ourselves knowledge of undiscovered life. We know only a fraction of the species on earth. Scientists have examined perhaps one out of every one hundred of earth's plant species and even fewer animal species.[76] There are no accurate figures on the number of species that exist (biologists guess anywhere from 5 to 30 million), or on rates of extinction. We do know that the tropics hold the greatest diversity. They cover only 7 percent of the earth's surface yet house 50–80 percent of the planet's species.[77] Tropical forests are being destroyed faster than any other area of the earth. Uncertainty is perhaps our greatest cause for alarm, both because we are engaging in yet another survival-threatening "experiment" with life on the planet and because there is a strong sense, especially among scientists, that we are permanently losing access to potential realms of knowledge.

The obvious connection to human welfare is that we use other species to sustain our own lives, primarily as food, but also as raw materials for industry and as sources for medicine. Over 25 percent of pharmaceuticals in use in the United States contain ingredients originally derived from wild plants.

Summary

We have tried to set out, as well as we can, a pessimistic but not worst-case scenario of the environmental issues that we face. We are not putting forward these views as "the facts" but are suggesting that they represent the possibility of an environmental crisis of significant proportion.

Notes

Chapter One

1. Woolard spoke at the Ariel Halperin Symposium at Dartmouth College in 1991.

2. Many others have come before us. We have especially benefited from conversations with Ed and Jean Stead and Paul Shrivastava. See especially W. Edward Stead and Jean Garner Stead, *Management for a Small Planet*, 2d ed. (Thousand Oaks, Calif.: Sage, 1996); and Paul Shrivastava, *Greening Business* (Cincinnati: Thompson Executive Press, 1996). Many others are attempting to bring together business and the environment, though in a fashion with which we have substantial disagreement. The best known is Paul Hawken, *The Ecology of Commerce* (New York: Harper, 1993), who argues that business must produce some harm that must be taxed to produce a sustainable economic system. We are in agreement with his idea that business can be transformational but not with the analysis and solutions that he offers. Others who have tried to pull these ideas together include Stephan Schmidheiny, *Changing Course* (Cambridge: MIT Press, 1992); Bruce W. Piasecki, *Corporate Environmental Strategy* (New York: Wiley, 1995); Frances Cairncross, *Costing the Earth* (London: Economist, 1991); Ernest Callenbach et al., *Ecomanagement* (San Francisco: Barrett Koehler, 1993); Thomas F.P. Sullivan, ed., *The Greening of American Business* (Rockville, Md.: Government Institutes, 1992); to name but a few. Two new scholarly journals have appeared, *Organizations and the Environment*, edited by John Jermier, and *Corporate Environmental Strategy*. There are a number of business organizations that support linking business and the environment. However, relatively few works, including those cited here, except for the Steads and Shrivastava, explicitly try to include ethics on an equal footing with business and the environment. Our argument is that all three are necessary.

3. We have no doubt that there can be and indeed are multiple conflicts.

These conflicts are a result of the conceptual schemes we have brought to bear on these issues. Our argument is that we need a new conceptual scheme, one that considers the possibility that these ideas can fit together. Arguments about what may be possible are fundamentally different from arguments that assess and judge what has been and is the case. By focusing on the possibility of how these ideas might work together, we hope to escape some of the morass that usually encumbers more academic arguments in business.

4. For a review of the literature on business ethics, see Patricia H. Werhane and R. Edward Freeman, "Business Ethics: The State of the Art," *International Journal of Management Research*, 1, no. 1 (1999) pp. 1–16.

5. Of course, these "business decisions" are moral in nature. The idea that business and morality have nothing to do with each other is called the Separation Thesis. If business is thought to be amoral and separate from ethics, and if ethics is thought to have nothing to say about the underlying process of value creation in society, then we have a logical explanation for why "business ethics" often appears as a joke. The Separation Thesis has long outlived any usefulness it may have had. See R. Edward Freeman, "The Politics of Stakeholder Theory," *Business Ethics Quarterly* 4, no. 4 (1994); and "Stakeholder Capitalism," *Financial Times*, July 26, 1996.

6. For a brief statement of the facts of the Exxon *Valdez*, see Patricia Bennett and R. Edward Freeman, "The Exxon Valdez" UVA-E-0085 (Charlottesville, University of Virginia, Darden Case Bibliography, 1995). For more in-depth analysis that is not particularly sympathetic to Exxon, see Art Davidson, *In the Wake of the Exxon Valdez* (San Francisco: Sierra Club Books, 1990).

7. The appendix to this book contains an analysis of the many facts pertinent to discussions of the environment.

8. Adam Smith was primarily concerned about justice.

9. A perfect example of this mind-set is Sharon Beder, *Global Spin: The Corporate Assault on Environmentalism* (Devon, VT: Green Books, 1997).

10. For a more careful analysis of this idea, see R. Edward Freeman, "The Business Sucks Story," Darden School of Business Working Paper no. 96–15 (Charlottesville: University of Virginia, 1996).

11. Pascal's wager does not work in its original form because it is a tenet of both Christianity and liberalism that individuals can decide for themselves whether to mortgage their own future in eternity for a few temporal moments of pleasure during life on earth. Our children's wager doesn't suffer from the same logical defect because the point is that our children will not get to make those choices if we do not begin to live differently. We have used "children" in the sense of future generations that include but may not be limited to existing children. For an analysis of Pascal's wager, see the volume of essays edited by Jeff Jordan, *Gambling on God: Essays on Pascal's Wager* (Lanham, Md.: Rowman & Littlefield, 1997).

12. For a canonical form of this argument, see Norman Myers and Julian Simon, *Scarcity or Abundance? A Debate on the Environment* (New York: Norton, 1994).

13. Combine this argument with the trend in many countries toward the devolution of government, and an increasing disenchantment with government as the solution rather than market mechanisms. The level of gridlock increases exponentially.

14. Our approach is radical—at least for business theorists and environmentalists. Most writing about the environment suggests that business is evil, and most writing on business suggests that business is separate from the environment. We want to stake out some new territory.

15. For an analysis of McDonald's restaurant chain, and its environmental strategy, see Susan Svoboda and Stuart Hart, "McDonald's/EDF: Cases Studies and Notes," National Pollution Prevention Center for Higher Education, Ann Arbor, MI: University of Michigan, 1995; for more general information on the history of the company, see John F. Love, *McDonald's: Behind the Arches* (New York: Bantam, 1995).

16. See Ralph Stayer, "How I Learned to Let My Workers Lead," *Harvard Business Review*, November-December 1990, pp. 66–83.

17. Note that this shift to values is not always in moral terms, even though Freeman and Gilbert argue that it should be. Many executives see these values as instrumental, leading to profits. We examine this idea in more detail in chapter 3.

18. The "what do you stand for" question is also known as "enterprise strategy" and is traceable to Peter Drucker. See R. Edward Freeman, *Strategic Management: A Stakeholder Approach* (Boston: Pitman, 1984).

19. See Michael Porter, *On Strategy* (Boston: Harvard Business School Press, 1998).

20. Portions of this chapter were published in *The Business of Consumption*, ed. Laura Westra and Patricia Werhane (Lanham, Md.: Rowman & Littlefield, 1998), pp. 339–353. We are grateful to the editors and publishers for allowing us to develop some of these ideas in that volume.

Chapter Two

1. These issues are explored in more depth in Robert Bruner et al., *The Portable MBA* (New York: Wiley, 1998), chap. 11, "Leading from the Middle."

2. Thus we are in agreement with the thrust of Tom Peter's analysis in his latest books, *Thriving on Chaos* (New York: Alfred A. Knopf, 1987) and *The Circle of Innovation* (New York: Alfred A. Knopf, 1997).

3. This section is based on R. Edward Freeman, "Stakeholder Capitalism," *Financial Times*, July 1996; and R. Edward Freeman and Jeanne Liedtka, "Stakeholder Capitalism and the Value Chain," *European Journal of*

Management, June 1997. We are grateful to the editors and publishers for permission to reprint some paragraphs and to recast others.

4. See Jim Collins and Jerry Poras, *Built to Last* (New York: Harper, 1995); and John Kotter and James Hesketh, *Corporate Culture and Performance* (New York: Free Press, 1992).

5. Defining narrow self-interest is a nontrivial topic. We believe that a proper understanding of the subtle distinctions in game theory and utility theory can do much to clarify these issues. For instance, see E. F. McClennen, *Rationality and Dynamic Choice* (Cambridge, U.K.: Cambridge University Press, 1995).

6. Cf. Collins and Porras, *Built to Last*.

7. Certain Asian economies have little competition even though the first three principles may be satisfied.

8. For a history of this idea, see R. Edward Freeman and Daniel R. Gilbert Jr., *Corporate Strategy and the Search for Ethics* (Englewood Cliffs, N.J.: Prentice-Hall, 1987).

9. The Merck story is told in Collins and Porras, *Built to Last*, and in Michael Useem, *The Leadership Moment* (New York: Random House, 1998). The original case study, done by the Business Enterprise Trust, is available from the trust or from the Harvard Business School Case Collection.

10. Collins and Porras, *Built to Last*, p. 68.

11. For an analysis of 3M, see Shrivastava, chapter 1 n. 2, pp. 149ff.

Chapter Three

1. Susan Svoboda and Stuart Hart, *McDonald's/EDF: Case Studies and Notes* (Ann Arbor: University of Michigan, National Pollution Prevention Center for Higher Education, 1995).

2. Alan Beckenstein et al., *Stakeholder Negotiations* (Chicago: Irwin, 1996).

3. Michael Porter, *On Strategy* (Boston: Harvard Business School Press, 1998). See, specifically, Michael Porter and Claas van der Linde, "Green and Competitive: Ending the Stalemate," *Harvard Business Review*, September-October 1995, pp. 120ff.

4. "Procter and Gamble," HBS 9-592-016 (Boston: Harvard Business, 1991).

5. "Selling of the Green; What's Good for the Planet Proves Good Business Too," *Chicago Tribune*, December 26, 1995.

6. " Power Shift," *Business Ethics*, May-June 1992, p. 18.

7. McDonald's views can be found on its Web site at www.mcdonalds.com. Information on the McDonald's EDF partnership can be found at www.edf.org/pubs/Reports/McDfinreport.html.

8. The British Petroleum *Annual Report on Environment, Health, and Safety* is available from the corporate offices in London.

9. See George Lodge, "Responsible Care," (Boston: Harvard Business School, 1991). Case 9-391-1135.

10. The Dupont statement can be found at *www.dupont.com/corp/gbl-company/she/commit.html.*

11. See Nevin Cohen et al., *Improving Dialogue: A Case Study of the Community Advisory Panel of Shell Oil Company's Martinez Manufacturing Complex* (New Bruswick, N.J.: Rutgers University, Center for Environmental Communications, 1995).

12. See "Conoco and the Rainforest" in Beckenstein et al., *Stakeholder Negotiations.*

13. John Elkington, "Towards the Sustainable Corporation: Win-Win-Win Business Strategies for Sustainable Development," *California Management Review,* Winter 1994, pp. 90–100.

14. Janet Bamford, "Changing Business as Usual," *Working Woman,* 18 (November 1993): 62–65.

15. Andrea Larson and Joel Reichart, "IKEA and the Natural Step," UVA-G-0501 Darden School Case Study (Charlottesville: University of Virginia, 1997).

16. J.A. Mast, ed., *Ward's Private Company Profiles* (Detroit: Gale, 1994), referring to E. O. Welles, "Lost in Patagonia," *INC.* 14, no. 8 (1992):44.

17. The source of these principles is William McDonough, "Industrial Revolution II," *Interiors and Sources,* May 1995. For more of McDonough's philosophy, see William McDonough, "A Boat for Thoreau: A Discourse on Ecology, Ethics, and the Making of Things," in *The Business of Consumption,* ed. Laura Westra and Patricia Werhane (Lanham, Md: Rowman & Littlefield, 1998).

18. Joan Magretta, "Growth through Global Sustainability: An Interview with Monsanto's CEO, Robert B. Shapiro," *Harvard Business Review,* January-February 1997, pp. 78–88.

19. For more information on Rohner Textile, see Mathew Mahalik, Michael Gorman, and Patricia Werhane, "Design Tex Inc. (A) and (B)," UVA E-099 (Charlottesville: University of Virginia, Darden Case Bibliography, 1996).

20. Edward D. Pasternack, "DMA Rodale Awards Honor Environmental Concern and Achievement," *Direct Marketing,* April 1996, pp. 18–24.

21. See www.agraquest.com.

Chapter Four

1. See, for example, Frederick Jackson Turner, *The Frontier in American Culture* (Tucson: University of Arizona Press, 1920); and Wendell Berry, *The Unsettling of America: Culture and Agriculture* (San Francisco: Sierra Club Books, 1977).

2. The publication of George Perkins Marsh's *Man and Nature* in 1864 was the first articulation in American writing of the idea that our way of life might have a negative impact on the earth. Marsh's book was the first to question whether nature's bounty really was limitless and to suggest that human lifestyles could negatively effect the balance of nature. It was many years

before his point took hold. See George Perkins Marsh, *Man and Nature*, ed. by David Lowenthal (Cambridge: Harvard University Press, 1965).

3. Gifford Pinchot, *Breaking New Ground* 1947; reprint (Seattle: University of Washington Press, 1972).

4. Samuel P. Hays, *Conservation and the Gospel of Efficiency* (Cambridge: Harvard University Press, 1959).

5. See, for example, Aaron Sachs, "Upholding Human Rights and Environmental Justice" in *State of the World 1996*, ed. Lester Brown et al. (New York: Norton, 1996), pp. 133ff.

6. Tom Regan, *The Case for Animal Rights* (Berkeley: University of California Press, 1984).

7. Arne Naess, *Ecology, Community, and Lifestyle*, trans. and ed. by David Rothenberg (Cambridge: Cambridge University Press, 1989).

8. Kirkpatrick Sale, *Dwellers in the Land: The Bioregional Vision* (San Francisco: Sierra Club Books, 1985).

Chapter Five

1. For an analysis of the importance of Deming's principles, see James A. Stoner, R. Edward Freeman, and Daniel R. Gilbert Jr., *Management*, 6th ed., (Englewood Cliffs, N.J.: Prentice-Hall, 1996), chap. 6.

2. John Kotter and James Hesketh, *Corporate Culture and Performance* (New York: Free Press, 1992).

3. See the references in chapter 1, footnote 2.

4. Stoner, Freeman, and Gilbert.

5. Ibid. Cit.

6. We are indebted here to Professors Jack Weber and Alec Horniman of the Darden School for many conversations about the ideas in this section. We are not claiming, as some do, that the future is totally independent of the past and therefore that anything is possible. Clearly, our ability to even imagine the future is connected to our understandings of our history and our institution's history.

7. Ernest Callenbach, *Ecotopia* (New York: Bantam Books, 1975); *Ecotopia Emerging* (Berkeley: Banyan Tree Books, 1981).

8. See, for instance, William Gibson, *Mona Lisa Overdrive* (New York: Bantam Books, 1989); Melissa Scott, *Dreamships* (New York: Tor, 1992); and Bruce Sterling, *Crystal Express* (New York: Ace, 1990).

9. Edward O. Wilson, "Is Humanity Suicidal?" *in People, Penguins, and Plastic Trees*, ed. Christine Pierce and Donald Van DeVeer, 2d ed. (Belmont: Wadsworth), 34–39.

10. For an analysis of the complicated issues surrounding biodiversity, see Edward O. Wilson, *The Diversity of Life* (Cambridge: Harvard University Press, 1992); Marjorie Reaka-Kudla, Don Wilson, and Edward O. Wilson, eds., *Biodiversity II: Understanding and Protecting Our Biological Resources*

(Washington, D.C.: Joseph Henry Press, 1997); and Niles Eldredge, *Life in the Balance: Humanity and the Biodiversity Crisis* (Princeton: Princeton University Press, 1998).

11. We warned you that this was an argument about possibility, not the standard one that suggests that we trade in our microwaves for toaster ovens, or that we go live in the woods on nuts and berries. It is our experience that environmentalists are no better than business executives when it comes to entertaining possibilities that have been little explored. It is not often the case that science fiction and the environment are mentioned in the same breath.

12. For an initial attempt to see human ethical obligation as just one more Darwinian process, see R. Edward Freeman and Joel Reichhert, "Towards a Life Centered Ethic," *Business Ethics Quarterly*, in press.

Appendix

1. There are many possible sources for the arguments in this appendix. For a good overview of the issues and current data on them, see *Global Environment Outlook*, United Nations Environment Program (New York: Oxford University Press); Lester R. Brown, Christopher Flavin, and Hilary French, *State of the World, 1998* (New York: Norton, 1998); and Lester R. Brown, Christopher Flavin, and Hilary French, *Vital Signs 1998* (New York: Norton, 1998).

2. Overpopulation is considered by many to be the cornerstone of a vast and threatening crisis. A bloated human population is straining the earth's life-support system, swallowing up resources, and clogging the earth with pollution and waste. The earth has a finite capacity to sustain life. Every person has a considerable impact in terms of the amount of energy and resources used and waste produced, and given the severity of our present environmental situation, additional strain on the earth in the form of expanding human numbers is something we cannot afford.

Overpopulation is directly linked to every one of the environmental issues outlined in this appendix. The human population is now estimated to exceed 5 billion, up from 1.5 billion one hundred years ago. The United Nations estimates a population of 6 billion in 2,000 and between 8 and 15 billion by the twenty-second century, when growth is expected to level off. The population growth rate has slowed slightly in the last decade, but the population explosion has not ended, especially since we now have a younger population and can expect still more children.

Quality of life will probably decline as numbers increase. By 2000, 1.7 billion people are projected to be living in countries that cannot support existing populations. Employment, education, shelter, and food already are not being provided for the current world population. Overpopulation lowers quality of life, not only because it contributes to environmental problems but also because it tends to create situations of political instability and social conflict.

The issues that overpopulation raises about social justice, human rights, and respect for life tend to discourage open discussion about whether or not the human species exists in overabundance. The subject carries a certain taboo in our society, fueled by groups who elicit images of imposed sterilization, forced abortions, "incentives" for having small families, and other draconian measures. As often as not, overpopulation drops out of the environmental conversation.

The issue of food or food security is connected to overpopulation rather directly. Our ability to produce food and the ways in which we go about this lie at the center of our environmental crisis. Feeding ourselves is our most fundamental occupation, and difficulties in this realm pose a basic threat. Demand for food grows as population expands. Between 1050 and 1984, thanks to the green revolution, world grain output increased dramatically. However, it has declined each year since 1984. The most obvious part of the food crisis is world hunger, the statistics on which are mind boggling. Some estimates place the number of deaths from hunger and hunger-related disease at 40–60 million people each year. United Nations agencies give a more conservative figure of 17 million deaths, 14 million being children. It is estimated that nearly a billion people do not consume enough calories for an active working life.

However, even population is not free from the kind of controversy that we mention in chapter 1. Julian Simon has developed an argument that it is the fact of population that will solve any environmental problem we may have. Human "smarts" are the only resource that matters, according to Simon, and the more the merrier. See Julian L. Simon, *The Ultimate Resource 2* (Princeton: Princeton University Press, 1996).

3. Natural Resources Defense Council, "Population and Consumption: Human Population Growth." Available at: www.labornet.org/nrdc/bkgrd/pogrow.html.

4. World Resources Institute, *World Resources 1994–95: A Guide to the Global Environment* (New York: Oxford University Press, 1994), p. 2.

5. L. Durrell, *State of the Ark: An Atlas of Conservation in Action* (London: Gaia, 1986), p. 32.

6. Whereas the "hazardous" category refers to materials that are dangerous in some way, "toxic" describes those that have direct biological impact, either acute or chronic.

7. Theo Colborn, Dianne Dumanoski, and John Peterson Myers, *Our Stolen Future* (New York: Penguin, 1996), pp. 89–90.

8. This means that they are not broken down easily by natural decay. Cf. Colborn, Dumanski, and Mayers, *Stolen Future*, p. 88.

9. J. Naar, *Design for a Liveable Planet* (New York: Harper & Row, 1990), p. 45; and G. Tyler Miller, *Living in the Environment: An Introduction to Environmental Science*, 6th ed. (Belmont, Calif: Wadsworth, 1990), p. 471.

Although Congress banned the manufacture of PCBs in 1976, thousands of tons had already entered the ecosystem through dumping in landfills, streams, sewers, and along roadsides.

10. Walter Corson, ed., *Global Ecology Handbook* (Boston: Beacon, 1990), p. 247.

11. Naar, n. 9, p. 44; and The World Resources Institute, *Environmental Almanac* (Boston: Houghton Mifflin, 1992) p. 89.

12. *Environmental Almanac*, pp. 33–49, 88–89; and Corson, *Global Ecology Handbook*, n. 10, pp. 247–253.

13. *Environmental Almanac*, p. 88, and Corson, p. 247.

14. Associated Press, "EPA Issues Proposed Standards for Reducing Radioactivity," *New York Times*, April 2, 1983.

15. Cf. Colborn, Dumanoski, and Myers, *Stolen Future*, p. 113.

16. See "Hazardous Substances, EPA Urges Lower Cancer Risk Estimate for Dioxin; Critics Charge Poor Science," *Daily Report for Executives*, June 30, 1988; R. Irvine and J. Goulden, "Ragged Response on Dioxin," *Washington Times*, August 22, 1991; "Environmentalist Groups Welcome EPA Response on Dioxin Policy, Call for Further Measures," *U.S. Newswire*, September 12, 1991; Colborn, Dumanoski, and Myers, *Stolen Future*, p. 116; and "Investigating the Next 'Silent Spring'," *U.S. News and World Report*, March 11, 1996, p. 50.

17. Corson, *Global Ecology Handbook*, p. 247.

18. The EPA report *Reordering Priorities?* shows chemical waste disposal to be a major public worry, though it was not considered a priority issue in the EPA's own ranking of human and environmental risks. M.B. Gerrard, *Whose Backyard, Whose Risk* (Boston: MIT Press, 1994).

19. Miller, *Living*, p. 477. Another estimate places the number of hazardous waste landfills at 15,000 with an additional 80,000 contaminated lagoons. Cf. Corson, *Global Ecology Handbook*, p. 248.

20. J. M. Moran, M. D. Morgan, and J. H. Wiersma, *Introduction to Environmental Science*, 2d ed. (New York: Freeman, 1989).

21. Fred Setterberg and Lonny Shavelson, *Toxic Nation* (New York: Wiley, 1993), p. 123.

22. "Haiti Returning Ash Dump to U.S.," *Chicago Tribune*, December 21, 1990.

23. Keith Schneider, "Opening the Record on Nuclear Risks," *New York Times*, December 3, 1989.

24. However, there is another source of nuclear waste that is often overlooked: the medical industry. Advocates of the nuclear defense industry point out that the ionizing radiation produced by nuclear testing is minimal compared to exposure from natural background sources like radon. One source gives the following figures for natural sources and human activities that contribute to the average amount of radiation received by the U.S. population: 54 percent from radon, 14 percent from medical X-rays and testing, 11

percent from air, food, and water, 8 percent from cosmic rays, 8 percent
from rocks and soil, 3 percent from other human sources, and 2 percent
from nuclear testing. Cf. Miller, *Living*, p. 452.

25. For an account of the Bhopal tragedy, see P. Shrivastava, *Managing Industrial Crisis: Lessons from Bhopal* (India: Vision Books, 1987).
26. K. Schneider, "California Spill Exposes Gaps in Rail Safety Rules," *New York Times*, July 27, 1991.
27. See National Resources Defense Council, "Effects of Chernobyl." Available at: www.labornet.org/nrdc/bkgrd/nucheref.html.
28. ABC Evening News, January 26, 1997.
29. P. Shabecoff, "The Rash of Tanker Spills Is Part of a Pattern of Thousands of Years," *New York Times*, June 29, 1989.
30. J. Leslie, *The End of the World* (London: Routledge, 1996).
31. Leslie, *End of the World*, p. 65.
32. "Government Concentrates," *Chemical and Engineering News*, April 22, 1996, p. 29.
33. Y.M. Ibrahim, "Most Oil Fires Are Out in Kuwait, But Its Environment Is Devastated," *New York Times*, October 19, 1991.
34. "Pesticide" is the imprecise term used to refer to various substances that kill or control pests. More specific terms are frequently used in discussions of the manufacture or regulation of these substances: an insecticide is a poison that kills or otherwise controls insects, an herbicide kills unwanted vegetation, a fungicide kills fungi, a rodenticide kills small animals, an avicide kills birds, an ovicide destroys eggs, and so on.
35. Corson, *Global Ecology Handbook*, p. 252.
36. George Ware, *The Pesticide Book* (St. Paul: Thomson Publishing, 1994).
37. Miller, *Living*, p. 557.
38. M. Burros, "New Urgency Fuels Effort to Improve Safety of Food," *New York Times*, May 7, 1990. The Federal Insecticide, Fungicide, and Rodenticide Act of 1972 is the only U.S. environmental law that allows substances known to be human carcinogens to be used when potential economic benefits are thought to outweigh the harms.
39. "Investigating the Next 'Silent Spring'," *U.S. News and World Report*, March 11, 1996, p. 51.
40. K. Schneider, "Deadly Pesticide May Face U.S. Ban," *New York Times*, March 26, 1991.
41. Jeff Wheelwright, "The Berry and the Poison," *Smithsonian*, December 1996, pp. 40–50.
42. M. Burros, "New Urgency Fuels Effort to Improve Safety of Food," *New York Times*, May 7, 1990.
43. W.H. Corson, ed., *Global Ecology Handbook*, p. 252. Postel quote.
44. Lois R. Ember, "Responsible Care: Chemical Makers Still Counting on It to Improve Image," *Chemical and Engineering News*, May 1995, pp. 10–12.

45. B. Breen, "Landfills are #1," *Garbage*, September-October 1990, p. 42.

46. Breen, "Landfills."

47. Available at: 1.brunel.ac.uk:8080/depts/chem/advanced/research/gill.htm.

48. *The Pollution of Lakes and Reservoirs*, UNEP Environment Library no. 12 (Nairobi: UN Environment Programme, 1994), p. 6.

49. Corson, *Global Ecology Handbook*, pp. 162–164; and *Environmental Almanac*, pp. 86–99.

50. *Pollution of Lakes and Reservoirs*, p. 15.

51. Corson, p. 165.

52. *Environmental Almanac*, p. 91.

53. A. Bredin, "On Ill Health and Air Pollution," *New York Times*, October 7, 1990.

54. Bredin, "On Ill Health."

55. Ibid.

56. U.S. Senate Subcommittee on Environmental Protection, *Hearing*, March 13, 1991, p. 2.

57. Miller, *Living*, p. 503.

58. Methane has been a source of considerable controversy and provides a good example of how unstable scientific "evidence" or argument on both sides of an issue can seem. The gas is produced by the decomposition of organic matter in landfills, swamps, cattle pens, and rice paddies. Some scientists view methane as one of the most serious hazards, especially given the rapid rates of increase in the past decade. Others say that methane cannot be considered an environmental problem, since it has always been around in large quantities. Some scientists think methane may not affect warming; others admit potential effects but say that concentrations are beginning to decrease.

59. U.S. Senate Subcommittee on Environmental Protection, *Hearing*, March 13, 1991, p. 2. CFCs are also the main actors in another environmental saga: depletion of the ozone layer. When CFCs rise to the stratosphere they release free chlorine, which destroys ozone.

60. John Houghton, *Global Warming: The Complete Briefing* (Cambridge: Cambridge University Press, 1997); S. George Philander, *Is the Temperature Rising? The Uncertain Science of Global Warming* (Princeton: Princeton University Press, 1998); C. Simon Silver with R. S. DeFries for the National Academy of Sciences, *One Earth, One Future: Our Changing Global Environment* (Washington, D.C.: National Academy Press, 1990). See also *Changing by Degrees: Steps to Reduce Greenhouse Gases* (Washington, D.C.: Office of Technology Assessment, 1991); and U.S. Senate Subcommittee on Environmental Protection, *Hearing*, March 13, 1991, p. 2.

61. *The Private Sector/Wise Use Memo* of February 1992 says that global warming is a false alarm. The president of the National Academy of Engineering is quoted as a source. The *Wise Use Memo* is published by the Center for the

Defense of Free Enterprise, an organization that spearheads the Wise Use movement.

62. B. McKibben, *The End of Nature* (New York: Anchor, 1989), p. 40; Corson, *Global Ecology Handbook*, p. 228.

63. "Ozone Science," USEPA and Ozone Depletion, available at: www.epa.gov/ozone/science/sc_fact.html.

64. "NASA Expedition Findings Predict Increased Ozone Depletion over Arctic," *International Environment Daily*, February 5, 1992.

65. B. Rensberger, "Ecology: Algae Growth Slows under Ozone Hole," *Washington Post*, February 24, 1992.

66. Norman Myers, *The Primary Source* (New York: Norton, 1984), p. 3.

67. Miller, *Living*, p. 222.

68. L. B. Stammer, "Study Finds Serious Harm to 10% of World's Best Soil," *Los Angeles Times*, March 25, 1992. The U.N. study estimated that overgrazing accounted for 35 percent of the world's degraded land, unsuitable agricultural practices for another 28 percent, and deforestation for 30 percent.

69. Myers, *The Primary Source*, p. 40.

70. Miller, *Living*, p. 288.

71. Myers, *The Primary Source*, p. 42.

72. Myers, *The Primary Source*, p. 42.

73. Quoted in *The Encroaching Desert: The Consequences of Human Failure; A Report for the Independent Commission on International Humanitarian Issues* (London: Zed, p. 20).

74. Myers, p. 46.

75. *Encroaching Desert*, p. 15.

76. The World Commission in Environment and Development, *Our Common Future* (New York: Oxford University Press), p. 147.

77. Niles Eldredge, *Life in the Balance: Humanity and the Biodiversity Crisis* (Princeton: Princeton University Press, 1998); Edward O. Wilson, *The Diversity of Life* (Cambridge: Harvard University Press, 1993); Marjoir L. Reaka-Kudla, Don E. Wilson, and Edward O. Wilson, eds., *Biodiversity II: Understanding and Protecting Our Biological Resources* (Washington, D.C.: Joseph Henry Press, 1997); E. Linden, "The Death of Birth," *Time*, January 2, 1989, p. 32.

Index

Enterprise strategy
  and corporate ethics, 11–12
  green framework for
    announcement of, 33–34
    development of, 32–33
    and innovative mind-set, 34–35
  greening of
    questions inherent in, 61–62
    techniques for, 37–39
  source of, 125n18
  in values-based capitalism
    business success and, 27–30
    creating and sustaining of, 30–31
    importance of having, 26–27
    innovation in, opening avenues for, 31
    questions asked in, 25–26
Environment
  current state of, 9
  gambling with, 8–9
  as stakeholder, 55–56
  value of, 5
Environmental action
  commitment to, 84, 86–87
  current, ineffectiveness of, 8–9
Environmental concepts, learning of. *See* Literacy, environmental
Environmental crisis
  business as solution to, 9, 112
  as catalyst of change, 82
  necessity of addressing, 2–3
  political institutions and, 25, 38
Environmental Defense Fund, 37, 52
Environmental effects, certainty of, as basic principle, 32–33
Environmental gridlock, 9
Environmentalism. *See also entries under* Green
  competition and, 16
  corporate, types and degrees of, 12–16, 38–39. *See also* Dark green; Light green; Market green; Stakeholder green
  cultural imperialism and, 79
  as expression of ethics, 16–17
  mental barriers to, 4–8

in new business environment, 21–22
and Quality movement, 83–84
value base of, learning about, 16–17
women and, 71
Environmentalists
  diversity of views among, 15–16, 78–79
  mind-sets among, 17
  values of, need to understand, 63–64
Environmental law, compliance with
  and good citizenship, 41
  as spur to innovation, 39–40
  vs. voluntarism, 51–52
Environmental Protection Agency (EPA)
  air standards and, 111, 112
  dioxin policy of, 100
  and pesticides, 105–106
  and radionuclides, 99
  and Resource Conservation and Recovery Act, 101–102
Environmental racism, 70
Environment issues, ubiquity of, 3–4
EPA. *See* Environmental Protection Agency
Ernst, Winter and Sohn, environmental programs of, 54–55
Ethics. *See also entries under* Values
  companies driven by, 6
  as foundation for new logic of business, 22–23
  good faith in, 16
  necessity of addressing, 2
  vs. profit, 2
  and responsibility, 33
  self-awareness in, 16
  Separation Thesis in, 124n5
Ethyl parathion, ban on, 106
Eutrophication, 109
Executives. *See* Business leaders
Extinction of species. *See* Biodiversity, loss of
Exxon *Valdez* oil spill, 104
  as milestone, 3

Facts, environmental
  need to know, for effective action, 68–69

Public policy. *See also* Government;
Regulation
 disagreements in, 9
 over-reliance on, as barrier to environmentalism, 4–5
Public policy process, inadequacies of, 9
Punishment of polluters, past, as cause
 of environmental gridlock, 9, 85,
 90–91

Quality movement, and environmental-
 ism, 83–84
Quality processes, logic of, 15
QVC (quality, value, and cleanliness), as
 McDonald's Corp. motto, 10

Radionuclides, as contaminant, 99–100
Rainforest Alliance, 55
Rainforest Cafe, Inc., 44
RCRA. *See* Resource Conservation and
 Recovery Act, 1976
Real Goods Trading Corp., 60–61
Recommended actions
 for individuals, 93
 for society, 90–92
Regulation(s). *See also* Government;
 Public policy
 of airborne pollutants, 112
 and competitiveness, 13
 compliance with, as business strategy, 13
 current, ineffectiveness of, 8–9
 of pesticides, 105–106
 political attempts to influence, 40
 poorly-conceived, 43
 problems with relying on, 4–5
 Resource Conservation and
  Recovery Act, 101–102
 as stakeholder interest alignment, 48
 strict, possibility of meeting, 1
 as threat to capitalism, 6–7
Regulatory mind-set, as barrier to environmentalism, 4–5
Reilly, William K., 100
Relentlessness
 as characteristic of innovative
  mind-set, 35

in implementation of change, 86–87
Religious organizations, and environ-
 mental action, 91–92
Religious values, and environmental
 education programs, 91
Resistance to change, 81–82, 86
Resource Conservation and Recovery
 Act, 1976 (RCRA), 101–102, 108
Respiratory ailments, air pollution and,
 112
Responsibility, principle of, in develop-
 ment of green framework, 32, 33
Responsible Care program, 51, 107
Rio Earth Summit (1992), 6
River blindness, Merck cure of, 26–27
Robert, Karl-Henrik, 56
Rocky Flats plant, 103
Rohner Textile, 60
Royal Dutch Shell, and minority rights,
 69

Sacramento River, chemical spill in
 (1991), 103
Schools and environmental action,
 91–92
Schumpeter, Joseph, 19, 20
Scott, Melissa, 85
In Search of Excellence (Peters and
 Waterman), 10, 24
Self-deception, definition of, 16
Self-interest, defining, 126n5
Separation Thesis, 124n5
Service to customers
 ethics of, 46–47
 support for, 47–48
Shell Oil, community responsiveness of,
 52
The Silent Spring (Carson), 105
Simon, Julian, 130n2
Slash-and-burn agriculture, effect of,
 118
Smith, Adam, 6
Smog, photochemical, 111
Socialist nations
 emerging capitalism in, 23
 failed policies of, 6–7
Social justice mind-set, 17